Being You

Maggie Eyre is an internationally recognized teacher and coach who has devoted her working life to help clients develop personal presence and leadership skills by boldly embracing their authentic selves. In recent years her quest has been to help people from all walks of life align their values and personal behaviour to create a consistent reputation and unique personal brand. Maggie's message is that we all have the power to create, manage and control the stories and images we share in the wider world. How well we do this is defined by self-awareness, consistency, confidence and integrity.

Maggie has over 30 years' experience as a professional performance trainer, personal coach and business woman. She trains senior business executives, prominent politicians, high-performance athletes and academics, helping them to unlock their true voices and shine on the stage. Maggie lives in Auckland where she runs Fresh Eyre, a unique presentations skills training and coaching company. Her previous book, *Speak Easy: The essential guide to speaking in public* (Exisle Publishing) is sold around the world.

To learn more about Maggie visit: www.maggieeyre.com

Being You

How to build your personal brand and confidence

Maggie Eyre

EXISLE
PUBLISHING

First published 2019

Exisle Publishing Pty Ltd
226 High Street, Dunedin, 9016, New Zealand
PO Box 864, Chatswood, NSW 2057, Australia
www.exislepublishing.com

A CiP record for this book is available from the National Library of Australia.

ISBN 978 1 925335 92 7

Designed by Enni Tuomisalo
Typeset in Droid Serif, 10pt
Printed in China

This book uses paper sourced under ISO 14001 guidelines from well-managed forests and other controlled sources.

10 9 8 7 6 5 4 3 2 1

Disclaimer

While this book is intended as a general information resource and all care has been taken in compiling the contents, neither the author nor the publisher and their distributors can be held responsible for any loss, claim or action that may arise from reliance on the information contained in this book. As each person and situation is unique, it is the responsibility of the reader to consult a qualified professional regarding their personal circumstances.

To my mum, Jean Violet Eyre.

You shaped my personal brand from the very beginning. You lived a life of sacrifice and integrity and always told the truth. Without knowing it, you were my guide and my teacher. I did not know what it meant to live an authentic life until your time in this world came to its end. Every day I miss you. Every day I try to live and work in your image.

Contents

Rt Hon Helen Clark

Foreword

I am delighted to recommend Maggie Eyre's new book: *Being You: How to build your personal brand and confidence.*

Maggie's view is that a personal brand tells the world who you are as a human being — both personally and professionally. While it's a lifetime exercise to build a personal brand, getting the key support, advice, and training in place early on is enormously important for self- confidence and future success.

Many seek advice on personal presence from those like Maggie who specialize in personal branding. Maggie's tips and techniques have long stood me in good stead. I have known Maggie for many years, both professionally and as a friend. I benefited a great deal from the support, help, and advice she gave me at an earlier stage of my political career when I had to deal with continual personal criticism which got in the way of delivering my message. With support from Maggie, I was able to work on my personal brand so that I could make my image a genuine reflection of who I was.

For me, idealism, a sense of purpose, and basic values of fairness and creating opportunity for all are central to what I stand for. I've always been passionate about working for change based on those values. Maggie's new book has a focus on social media which, these days, is important in conveying values and direction, and, thus, in building a personal brand. I myself am active on social media platforms.

I believe much of my success has related to having a message based on my basic values. To do that well, I need to maintain ownership and continual quality control over what I say and how I say it. That holds true for everything I do in the public arena — whether it's a media interview, a meeting, or a presentation. Like Maggie, I believe that how one presents in all forums needs to be consistent with one's core beliefs and values.

Being You will show you how to build a holistic, genuine and authentic personal brand across everything you do. Therefore, I strongly recommend *Being You* to people who are committed to making their mark on our world, whatever their field of endeavour may be. I hope that others will benefit, as I did, from taking the advice which Maggie offers — it is globally relevant, and it should be heeded!

Helen Clark

Former Prime Minister of New Zealand

Former Administrator of the United Nations Development Programme

Introduction

66 One of the sad things today is that so many people
    are frightened by the wonder of their own presence.
    They are dying to tie themselves into a system, a role,
    or to an image, or to a pre-determined identity that
    other people have actually settled on for them."
    —*John O'Donohue, Irish philosopher*[1]

Imagine it's the last day of your working life. The last log off has been completed and the last hand has been shaken. You are surveying your career and remembering the days and years of making and creating something that filled you with purpose and pride. The mistakes you made have been embraced and overcome in a life punctuated by courage and integrity. In looking back, you know you have honoured yourself, made a contribution to everyone you worked with and touched people's lives in unique and unexpected ways. Your legacy is a rich tapestry of achievement after a life lived in step with your values, with firm footprints paved for others to follow in. Your reputation, or 'brand', is intact.

The buzz phrase 'personal branding' used to drive me nuts. And yet, I began to catch myself using this term consistently when working with my clients in daily coaching sessions, in the training workshops I led, in speeches I delivered and the everyday running of my company, Fresh Eyre. I had always thought there were more than enough books, social media articles and presentations about personal branding. So I was surprised when the nagging chitter chatter in my mind persisted with the questions, 'What can I say about personal branding that is different? What do I know and could share with others?' As it turns out, I've had an abundance of experience in growing my own successful brand and helping others grow theirs, so I thought it was time for me to join the conversation with my own unique perspectives and usual candour.

I have had endless conversations with friends and clients and given many workshops and presentations about personal branding. I hear quite regularly how people dislike the term 'personal branding' and frankly, I get that and nod in agreement. It's much maligned, however, because too often the concept of personal branding is used cynically by people to lie, manipulate, self-promote and sell untruths. Making this distinction is a good learning point and I hope you will be challenged in this book to see personal branding as an opportunity to be fully and authentically expressed, which is the opposite of manipulative self-promotion in which one markets and sells a fake person or product.

During many conversations with my publisher, friends and clients, I strung together an outline for how I would approach a book on building your personal brand. In these chats, the word that continued to emerge as a guiding beacon was authenticity. It was a word that framed all my thinking because, at my core, I believe it's the best currency to trade in when growing a personal brand. For many, being honest and authentic all the time is not easy because we don't want to hurt other people's feelings or feel uncomfortable. Let's face it, it's risky being authentic and transparent. Not everyone enjoys being around people who are sincerely frank and honest. Being yourself can be irritating to others so it's no wonder many people 'fake it' and give the world a distorted version of their true selves.

In recent years, I have embarked on many discussions about the times in my life when I was being inauthentic and have shared with clients about how, in owning that inauthenticity, I have profoundly changed. It was my big brother, Tony, who helped me to examine my relationship with authenticity and led me to embark upon a challenging journey of rediscovering myself as a 'brand' in the world. In 2016, he watched me in a short television interview on a breakfast show and said it was the most authentic interview he had seen me do. He told me I looked more like myself and that I was relaxed, conversational and honest. This critique segued into him candidly sharing with me how, in earlier television and radio interviews in my career, he'd found me inauthentic.

It takes immense courage and care to give feedback to someone you love, especially family, and it never occurred to me that I had been 'performing' in hundreds of interviews. I trained as a professional actress in my twenties, so performance comes naturally to me. But Tony's feedback caused me to pause and reflect. Nowadays, I stand back and analyze my media interviews and presentations with a fresh eye and always ask myself, 'Did I come across as authentic? Was I being real in that moment? Was this interview good for my personal brand?' After all, being a student in life is part of my philosophy.

I have dedicated my entire life's work to studying and understanding communication. Like most trained actors, communication is what I am good at and I feel confident and at ease when being interviewed by the media, giving keynote speeches and leading workshops in many countries around the world. I'm a passionate performer and these days I am also a rigorously authentic one. I share my knowledge and stories on whatever stage I find myself, whether it be corporate or creative; academic or altruistic. I try to add value in any way I can and to anyone. And I use tools from my careers in teaching, acting, publicizing, public relations, presentation skills coaching and corporate team-building. For instance, I rummage through my 'actor's kit' to use relevant tools to teach people how to open up and be expressive. As a professional actress, it was my joy to learn about human behaviour, body language, the voice and the emotion behind words. It was my job to think about the messages (and subtext) behind every single sentence, short or long. These insights come into focus when working with clients to better perform in their jobs, while also encouraging them to embrace their vulnerabilities as strengths and not weaknesses.

Developing a personal brand is a bit like developing a personal style. This book shares stories about my client work and shows you, the reader, how to grow your personal brand. I hope some of the stories resonate and are easily relatable to your own experiences and challenges. It's my intention to pass on useful tips and strategies that will help you build or refresh your personal brand and encourage you to be more genuine when communicating. In these pages, I will remind you about the importance of 'being real' and 'being yourself' with the people in your life. We spend most of our days talking and listening to others, but rarely have the time to think about how we are being perceived. First impressions matter and this book will show you the necessary steps to make a good impression in your personal brand.

Many brave and generous colleagues and clients have given me permission to share their stories in this book. You will read about ordinary and extraordinary people I have met, observed and worked with, all of whom have managed their brands with great credit. I have studied and researched for over 30 years in this field and I have been privileged to watch people transform their lives in my workshops and in regular ongoing training sessions.

Staying true to your values requires a strong sense of self-belief. When I was younger, my standards were impossibly high, and in my mind I was never good enough. I wanted approval from others, especially my peers in corporate jobs. Today, I continue to have high expectations of myself but I have a maturity that escaped me back then. I know that I'm my best critic because I know who I am now. The only person I need approval from is myself. And the same goes for you. Saying that, do keep on asking people you trust to give you feedback about your personal brand. Life does not have to be a one man/woman show. And your audience, especially these days with social media, is vast and wide.

A close friend once asked me, 'When are you going to start telling your real story?' I had spent a huge chunk of my early career protecting my privacy and shunning media interviews. I sometimes, not even consciously, chose to fly, if not below the radar, well below the altitude that was within my capability. Communicating my brand with the world online was something I had shied away from. With my friend's question ringing in my ears, I decided to respond. And what came out was the word 'Now!' It was time to further grow my brand and walk my talk. Would the real Maggie Eyre please stand up — and stand up now!

So, let me ask you the very same question: *When are you going to start telling your real story?* Do you think in your life and work you are fully expressed and, if not, what is it going to take to make that happen? What and who do you reveal in your work and play? And are you showing us the truth?

Whether you like it or not, you are a brand so why not do your best to present the 'authentic' you in your personal and professional life? Why not invest more time in making sure people get to know what makes you tick? We teach people how to treat us, so consider how much more satisfying your life could be if you projected the real you to others. Imagine a life without self-doubt and a stronger personal brand that speaks loudly about your beliefs and vision for a happier world. Imagine your days filled with stimulation and joy because people respected you for who you were — an introvert, an extrovert, a conservative, a feminist, a creative, a spiritual, an eccentric, a political, a maverick, a *bon vivant*, a corporate or an activist.

It does not matter who you are or what you do. When you speak your truth and act with great integrity and purpose, you inspire others and ignite hope. This is the stuff and making of great men and women, living big and voluptuous lives. It's also the stuff of unforgettable personal brands.

66   Today you are you, that is truer than true.
    There is no one alive who is youer than you!'[2]
    —*Dr Seuss*

1

What is a personal brand?

66 The keys to brand success are self-definition, transparency, authenticity, and accountability."

—*Simon Mainwaring, social media specialist and author*[1]

A personal brand tells the world about who you are as a human being personally and professionally. A personal brand is about authenticity and is derived exclusively from your mind, your heart, your values, your passions, your imaginings and what you believe to be true at the core of your personal and professional self. That's why it's unique — because it begins with and is created from the very original place/being which is you.

A personal brand will reveal everything about what your mission is in the world, which is formed from your true values. It finds expression in the words you use, the commitments you make and keep and the steadfast delivery of your word. What your body language says, what your voice says and the words you choose will shape your personal brand from the first impression you make, whether in the room, online or on the phone, right until final delivery and beyond.

Sadly, the term personal brand is often confused with blatant self-promotion and/or a cynical way to market oneself as something one is not, often to grab the spotlight, go viral, create a traditional and social media buzz and make a huge amount of money. In the pages of this book you will understand how and why a genuinely authentic and long-term successful personal brand is far from that commercial branding construct. You will learn how to think about it and then creatively cultivate and maintain your own particular and unique personal brand.

Here's a list of some public figures that make my list of genuinely credible and successful personal brands. It's not a statement of whether I like them or not, believe in what they believe, support them in the sporting arena or even like their work. But I am very clear about who these people are, their body of work, their values and the language they use to express their life's passions and missions.

- Oprah
- Michelle Obama
- Malala Yousafzai

- Meryl Streep
- Vivienne Westwood
- The Dalai Lama
- Roger Federer
- George Clooney

Exercise

Make a list of people you would describe as having a clear and successful personal brand and think about why and how they have achieved this.

Example: Malala Yousafzai is a Pakistani activist for female education and became the youngest Nobel Prize laureate when she was just seventeen years old. Malala has a global presence on the world stage. After being shot in the head by the Taliban for standing up for women's education, she decided to tell her story to help other young women. It was never her intention to build her personal brand but her speech at the United Nations in 2013 and her courageous fight to educate females of all cultures and creeds, resulted in her winning the Nobel Prize. I respect her because she used something that happened to her to highlight the plight of other young women and stand up for human rights. 'I tell my story,' she has said, 'not because it is unique, but because it is not. It is the story of so many girls.'

Imagining a personal brand

In beginning to think about your personal brand, there are three questions to pose and investigate.

- What is your authentic self?
- What is your reputation?
- What is your legacy?

Let's look at each of these questions in more detail.

Authenticity

> **"** To be nobody but yourself — in a world which is doing its best, night and day, to make you like everybody else — means to fight the hardest battle which any human being can fight, and never stop fighting."
>
> —*e.e. cummings, American poet, essayist, author and playwright*[2]

It's important to know who you are when building a personal brand because you need to know your strengths and weaknesses to confidently grow. *The Oxford English Dictionary* definition of authentic is: 'Of undisputed origin and not a copy; genuine.'[3] If you know who you are, you will stand by your values and begin to honestly express and radiate your beliefs. The only way to change behaviours is to understand how and why you behave across a range of scenarios in your life. Through living your values, you will be seen as somebody who is clear about what matters and you'll inspire people's confidence and trust in you and your brand. I know, from years of experience, that when going into a pitch meeting for the first time with a new client, the most successful thing I can do is to make sure I'm building a relationship with that client; I'm not in there selling. I need to fully understand who the client is and what their goals are.

Exercise

Write down three words that describe you and your personality. For instance, the words I would choose to describe myself are:

- open
- loyal
- caring.

Now ask a close friend or co-worker to choose three words to describe you. My personal assistant offered these words to describe me:

- vibrant
- empathetic
- honest.

People perceive us differently, often in ways we don't realize. A good way to discover how you are perceived and how authentic you are in both your personal and professional life is to get feedback from others. Be brave and start asking people how they perceive you. You'll learn a lot!

I interviewed a number of clients who are also my friends and I have chosen these two interviews to share because we've had long working relationships and they know me well. I asked the same question of all: 'How do see me?' Here are the responses.

Interview one

- 'You are courageous and take people as you find them.'
- 'You disregard people's normal boundaries — you get right in there.'
- 'You have the capacity to enter into people's experiences.'

Interview two

- 'You are energetic, deeply committed and enthusiastic about possibility.'
- 'You are like a light — the room becomes the brighter when you come into it.'
- 'You are focused and professional with a disciplined way of working.'

Reputation

It's human nature to judge and critique, so your reputation walks in the door often before you do. *The Oxford English Dictionary* definition of reputation is: 'The beliefs or opinions that are generally held about someone or something.'[4] In all parts of your life, whether it is business, dating or at a social event, people are constantly researching and asking around about you. You can't cover up a bad reputation with a beautiful dress or a pristine suit. You are the sum story of all your past actions, so what's inside you counts and how you have treated people is like an unprinted business card that has already been handed around. Thinking about your reputation is also important because you get to be in charge of creating how you want to live and act. You can map out your future mindfully and with great awareness rather than bumbling your way through another murky year and then another murky decade. If you treat people with disrespect or dishonesty the rumour mill will swiftly ignite and in this age of social media, your global reputation can be in tatters in a nanosecond. In this technological age, I cannot stress how carefully we need to act at all times to cultivate a fair, accurate and positive reputation. You cannot control people's minds and prejudices, but you can determine how you want your reputation and thus your brand to be perceived.

Exercise

Write down what you think your reputation is now, either personally or professionally. It could be in your marriage/relationship, in your household or in your workplace. Then write down what you want it to be. Notice the differences.

Ask yourself what the steps and actions are that you need to take to build the bridge between what your reputation is now and what it could become.

Legacy

Your legacy is different to your reputation. Reputation is how others perceive you now and how you have been perceived in the past. But your legacy is what you want to leave behind.

Your legacy revolves around your actions and how they influence your future. Part of my work is to help senior managers or CEOs exit their organizations and help them focus on branding to find new positions. Clients seem to find it useful when I ask the following confronting questions:

- 'What do you want your legacy to be when you leave this job?'

- 'Do you want to leave behind unfinished business, or do you want to be described as a hero who played a big game then left with ease, grace and professionalism?'

- 'What are the words you want your co-workers to use when they remember you?'

Exercise

When you are gone, how do you want people to remember you? On my gravestone I want the words, 'Maggie made a difference in the world'. Think of a few leaders who are no longer living and think about what they left behind. For example, Einstein not only left behind his scientific breakthroughs but the belief that science has a moral responsibility to humanity. Freedom fighter Nelson Mandela showed no bitterness after 25 years in prison and continued to stand for racial equality and reconciliation until his death. Pioneer Amelia Earhart showed us that women can do anything men can do when they pursue their talents and passions.

What are you building to leave behind? Make a list and review it daily.

> 66 Build a good name. Keep your name clear. Don't make compromises, don't worry about making a bunch of money or being successful — be concerned with doing good work and make the right choices and protect your work. And if you build a good name, eventually that name will be its own currency."[5]
>
> —*William Burroughs' advice to Patti Smith*

We can learn so much from looking at other people's personal brands, even if their work or beliefs are completely different from our own. Drawing inspiration from people's varied lives and stories stretches our imagination and inspires us to invest more time in our own personal brand. This has certainly been my own experience. Research takes time but makes us think about what we want and how we want to be seen in the world.

Below are four personal brands that interest me. I hope these case studies will be useful for you to examine and reflect upon as you think about your own unique brand.

Sharon Isbin, classical guitarist

> 66 In the guitar world, I always had to fight as a woman. In the music world I always had to fight as a guitarist."[6]

Sharon Isbin is a Grammy Award-winning classical guitarist living in New York City. Sharon is an artist of international acclaim and I have watched how she's grown her brand over the years with interest and admiration. By using Sharon as an example of a talented woman who has built a stellar career and successful personal brand, I hope you'll be inspired to generate ideas for your own branding journey. You may even want to write notes for each key point below.

Sharon started studying guitar in Italy when she was nine years old and was taught by some of the great maestros of classical guitar. Because of her standout talent, her father made a pact with her that she could only indulge her passion of launching model rockets in the backyard if she practised guitar for one hour every day. Sharon went on to become an expert in her field as a classical guitar soloist. She now plays sold-out shows all over the world and has been invited to perform with more than 170 orchestras.

Sharon was praised in 2014 by *Boston* magazine as 'the pre-eminent guitarist of our time'. She founded the guitar department at the Julliard School in New York in 1989 and two years later she received her first Grammy. No female guitarist has been recognized by the Recording Academy since. Her personal brand is exceptionally strong and many of her interviews tell a story of a committed trailblazer in her field who has paved the way, especially for women in a once traditionally male-dominated industry. A key message comes through in Sharon's interviews, which is, 'I never give up'. She is a role model for all those little girls out there who have a big dream.

Authenticity

When I watch and listen to Sharon talk in her media interviews, I see and experience someone who is down to earth and genuine in every way. I see a confident, positive, calm woman who freely expresses herself and is at ease in the public eye. I know this by studying her body language, listening to her voice and focusing on her storytelling and key messages. Whether onstage or being filmed relaxing and chatting in her Manhattan apartment, her clothing and the image she conveys oozes ease and authenticity.

Sharon's body language is natural and she always smiles when talking. This projects warmth. She's also a very good listener when being interviewed or in a conversation. Sharon has presence. When she enters a room to play her guitar she walks with good posture and has an aura of grace about her. Her style is feminine, glamorous and chic and she radiates beauty whether she's dressed for a performance or looking casual in boots and jeans. Her voice has a rich tone and is passionate and energetic. I can tell she loves what she does because of her enthusiasm in her vocal projection.

The inspiring documentary *Sharon Isbin: Troubadour*, which was watched by millions of people on television across the United States, gives a glimpse into Sharon's personality and life. (You can find excerpts online, which leave you wanting to know more about this formidable artist; you might even be able to track down a copy of the documentary.) Above all, it's her work that entices and compels. Listening to her music transports me to a peaceful world and soothes and stimulates even though I have little understanding of classical guitar. All I know is that I am in the presence of mastery!

Reputation

Sharon's reputation in the classical music world is of perfection. She has positioned herself at the top of her field with extraordinary technique and ability. Credible testimonials endorse her personal brand, with high-profile personalities like legendary musician Joan Baez and tennis champion Martina Navratilova singing her praises. It doesn't get any better than having former First Lady Michelle Obama introducing her at the White House for a private concert. Not bad for a little girl born in St Louis Park, Minnesota, who wanted to be a rocket scientist when she grew up. Discipline and determination were in her DNA from childhood, making her an example of what can happen if you apply yourself daily to your passion.

Her courage coming out as a lesbian in *Out* magazine in 1995 was discouraged by her manager. But with openly gay musicians like K.D. Lang and Melissa Etheridge rising to success, Sharon was determined to be true to her sexuality and speak freely about issues like same-sex marriage. She knows and lives her values and is unafraid to speak out and use her fame to help others be true to themselves.

Sharon is not only an icon as a classical guitarist but a well-balanced woman who eats healthy food and jogs frequently to allow for a healthy mind and body. In a feature profile published in the *New York Times*, Sharon's art, humanity and lifestyle was communicated in words and pictures, where we got to see photos of her in a dance class and eating at her favourite local organic restaurant with a friend.

Her disciplined life is also evident with a photo of her meditating in her Upper West Side apartment, a practice she has upheld since she was seventeen years old.

Legacy

Sharon's lasting legacy (in my opinion) will be as an example of someone who was a high-performing musician, teacher and role model to younger women, showing them they can achieve their dreams if they believe in who they are and work hard. Her legacy also will forever live in the practice rooms of Julliard and in its future graduates, who'll benefit from her founding the guitar department and establishing various degrees and diplomas.

Brand drives business

Sharon's presence on all social media platforms is powerful, warm and friendly and she comes across as approachable and fun. Her online footprint has made her brand more successful because it's visual — we get to see her playing guitar even on her Sundays off, collaborating with fellow maestros and we also see precious memorable moments at her concerts. Sharon has a following of fans and admirers who show up to her live international concerts, which consolidates and builds her network. What makes her brand successful is not just her talent. The marketing of her personal brand includes an up-to-date tour calendar, latest albums and recordings and regular postings of media interviews.

Brainstorming the Sharon Isbin brand

- Her brand is about musical mastery, beauty, professionalism, integrity, discipline and courage.

- She helps people by being herself. By coming out at an early age, she encourages others to do so too.

- She shares personal stories about her life.

- She grows her students and gives credibility to the art of classical guitar.

- Her brand is good for classical guitar as she brings ease, effortlessness and elegance to the musical world.

- She gives back by teaching young students and building programs for classical guitarists at a world-renowned performing arts school.

- She is comfortable in herself and her personality shines. She is healthy and looks after her wellbeing. She is likeable, unpretentious and believable.

Roger Federer, tennis champion

66 There is no way around hard work. Embrace it."[7]

Born in 1981 in Switzerland, Roger Federer became the top junior tennis player in his country by the age of eleven. In 1998, he fully committed to a career in tennis and turned professional. Five years later, he won Wimbledon and became the first Swiss man to win a Grand Slam singles title. Since then he has won more Grand Slam singles than any man in history.

Roger Federer's successful personal brand, valued at US$37 million a year, ranks among the highest earning brands in sport (according to Forbes Fab 40). He's affiliated with expensive high-end companies such as Nike, Rolex, Mercedes-Benz, Moët & Chandon and Credit Suisse. Fans follow and admire him from all corners of the world, especially tennis players who are inspired by not only his technique and match skills but his dedication and longevity. Federer just never gives up. Despite years of lower rankings and struggling to win a Grand Slam, Federer regained his form and again held trophies over his head. For this reason, his brand is associated with endurance as well as high performance and success. He is quite simply a legend of his sport.

The Roger Federer Foundation, backed by Credit Suisse, was set up in southern Africa in 2003 to support children in their early education. His passion for the developing countries of Africa was encouraged by his mother, Lynette, who was born in South Africa. At seven months old Federer was cradled by his mother on his first vacation to South Africa and during his childhood they visited relatives every two years with his sister and father, forming a strong bond with his mother's roots.

He talks openly in the media about his intention to continue his hands-on support of his foundation. What drew me to his personal brand was his philanthropic values and his sharing through interviews about his love for the poorest in Africa. 'This gigantic continent holds a magical attraction for me. A good education is something that nobody can take away,' said Federer.[8] His values shine through in both his speech and actions. Giving his name to the educational foundation adds kudos and credibility.

Before I researched Federer, I thought of him as a privileged man who had perfection written all over his personal luxury brand. But I was only focusing on his tennis fame and competence. A personal brand is made up of all of you and takes a 360-degree scope of your life. Federer is about high performance and high-end elegance but his powerful personal brand is underpinned by his reputation as a man of family, with his solid marriage and children, and a man of generosity, through his philanthropic work.

Authenticity

Is there such a thing as an authentic smile? Look no further than Roger Federer — his smile seems the same today as it was in the baby pictures on his blog. I've never seen a fake smile from this sports legend. If you study Federer's photos and television interviews online, you get to see how a genuine smile helps people warm to you and listen to what you have to say. Federer's smile encourages us to smile back; he seems at peace with himself in interviews.

Looking at Federer's on- and off-court body language in photographs and videos, there's a consistency of style and manner that underpins his brand — he is the ultimate professional, ever competitive, and yet elegant and almost exquisite in top form. For tennis lovers, King Roger or the Fed-Ex has an on-court style to die for. His serve is a master class in athleticism. When he's not on form he knows how to assess lesser performances with honesty and humility. He never bags the opposition or the referee, doesn't throw tantrums when things go wrong, and knows how to acknowledge his own success and the success of others — brilliantly.

A magic Federer moment, recorded on YouTube, is in the 2017 Laver Cup where he and Rafael Nadal (usually rivals) played together for the first time, against the US doubles combo of Sam Querrey and Denis Sock. The sheer joy of watching these two world champions having fun playing together, almost as brothers (and 'taking home' the game) is quite contagious and really special. There's no ego here, just authentic excellence.

Off the court, Federer's genuine warmth and consistency is equally present. An online video of him visiting a school he supports in Malawi is testament to his spontaneity, allowing us to see young disadvantaged African children touching the hair on his arms and him smiling back. He's almost cute and so natural!

For all his fame, income and success, Federer appears egoless and remains in touch with his own compassion and humanity. A classic example is the tweet he posted about the terrorist attacks in Mumbai in 2008. His message was heartfelt, touching and definitely aligned with his values.

One of Federer's great quotes is, 'You need a defeat to give value to your victories'. He always appears to be very real and sincere about his injuries and when he talks about his losses, tough times and mistakes he focuses on what he has learnt from errors. A consummate professional.

Reputation

Think of Brand Federer and you think of an unstoppable and unflappable athlete as well as a gentleman of the sport. He is gracious in winning and losing, and although he's ambitious, he never appears ruthless. Federer is renowned for his good manners and impeccable on-court behaviour, which adds to his elegant and composed image. It's no wonder he is so attractive for luxury brands to align themselves with. He fits them as well as they fit him.

Federer is known as a devoted husband to former tennis player Mirka and father to two sets of identical twins. Once a top-100 tennis player, Mirka retired from the game in 2002 after an ongoing persistent injury. Federer speaks lovingly about his partner in interviews and acknowledges his wife and family as a reason for his success both on and off the court. We get a sense of a happy, respectful marriage that helps any personal brand look good. Federer's wife worked as his PR manager for a time, which suggests to me a tight and trusting team. Federer says, 'Mirka has been an amazing support for me. She's been the best.'[9] Fans and followers of any personal brand want to know about human relationships, and at every Grand Slam there is Mirka sitting courtside, sometimes with the children. This suggests loyalty, unity and commitment, which adds to Federer's solid branding.

His high-profile charity work also enhances his reputation as being a 'good guy' of sport. It nicely balances out his endorsement of all things luxurious and protects him from accusations of being spoiled by a life of pomp and privilege.

Legacy

Roger the Great, Roger the Legend! This is without question how Federer will be remembered. Already, many commentators refer to him as the greatest male tennis player of all time. The annals of sporting history will forever proclaim the talents, endurance and comportment of Roger Federer. Even after his retirement, I will look forward to seeing him gracing stadiums around the world as an ambassador for the sport, to present and honour new champions as well as inspire and motivate through public-speaking engagements.

The Roger Federer Foundation will live on and this, in my opinion, will be his greatest legacy, as it touches millions of children's lives by helping them to have an education. His foundation gives children choices and they will forever be grateful to this tennis great. Having a foundation named after you gives a long life to any personal brand.

Children who spend many hours on the tennis court will be motivated to take risks and aspire to Federer's heights. I believe he will go down in history as not just one of the finest tennis players, but one of the finest athletes in the world.

Brand drives business

Federer's relationships and partnerships with exclusive and powerful brands raise the bar and lend further strength to his personal brand. He's an example of why you need to ask the questions, 'Who can I associate with to grow my personal brand?' and 'Who can endorse me with credible testimonials?'

Federer could easily set up an academy teaching anyone in business how to master the art of quality customer service, as he knows how to look after his followers, fans and global audiences. He could also offer us a masterclass on how to move on faster after failure rather than dwelling on not winning. In Federer's own words, 'I have more perspective. You absorb losses faster and easier, even though it hurts. You move on with it. You know you were well prepared, you know you tried your best. Rather than wasting negative energy on something you can't change anyway, you take it on the chin, you learn from it and move on.'[10]

One of the many lessons we can learn from Federer is to adapt and find new solutions in business when things go wrong. After severe injuries and losses on the court, Federer found new ways and strategies to play his game, returning stronger and more skilful. We can all do the same when the going gets tough.

Federer wears his own clothing range, generating sales by displaying his brand in front of millions, reminding fans to buy and wear it. Like his brand, the RF logo is refined and easy to recognize. It's nothing fancy; rather, it's a sophisticated scribble that sits perfectly on his garments and products. Our logos are a part of our branding and we need to get it right, as anything visual (like clothing) has a language.

Loyalty drives your business, as people keep on returning and waiting to see the best in action. Thousands of tennis fanatics put Federer's tournaments in their calendar well in advance and he's supported by a loyal base of 'Team Federer', which follows him around the world. Plainly put, Federer is a world-class mentor and an ambassador for excellence. He waves the flag for us to keep on striving against all odds. We need strong, courageous personal brands to motivate us, not just on the court but in life. In listening to high-performance athletes like Federer, we are compelled to try harder, work smarter and invest more time and commitment into our preparation.

Another lesson from Federer is that we must focus on our relationships with clients and customers and not focus on our competition. Federer focuses on the ball and not his opponent, with one goal only, which is to win. How often do we let our personal brand down by worrying about our competition and getting distracted? How often do we take our eyes off the ball? Sport is a valuable metaphor.

Federer's meaningful work with his charitable foundation enriches his personal brand around social responsibility while genuinely transforming communities in Africa. Lending your name and giving away hours to help the disadvantaged is deeply rewarding to those who receive but also to those who give. Federer cares about social justice and equality and his passion for the Roger Federer Foundation is evidence of this.

Social media has been a big part of Federer's successful brand since 2013 and is helped by tweeting once a day. With 28 million Twitter followers, his use of social media has increased his fan base and brand awareness, and has given him direct access to people interested in his story both on and off the court. No matter how big a sports superstar you are or how many times you raise the trophy in triumph, without a social media strategy and presence, your game in the branding arena will keep you confined to the early rounds.

Brainstorming the Roger Federer brand

- His personal brand successfully attracts high-end luxury brands like Rolex and Mercedes.
- He lives his mother's values and influences his children's relationships.
- He shares his earnings with children who are born into poverty in Africa.
- He grows his brand through regular posts through social media.
- He gives back to the community through his charitable trust.
- He is unique and has achieved unmatched success in his sport.
- He endures and inspires us to never give up.

Ed Sheeran, singer and songwriter

❝ I can't tell you the key to success, but the key
to failure is trying to please everyone."[11]

Ed Sheeran was born in West Yorkshire but grew up in Suffolk, England, in a small town of less than 5000 people. He was part of a supportive and creative family, with one older brother. He started singing and playing his guitar at the age of eleven while also singing in the church choir. Ed dropped out of school when he was sixteen, with a passion to pursue music. Initially he did some busking on the streets to earn money while independently publishing his early recordings. For a few years, Ed had no fixed address and even slept rough on the London streets some nights near Buckingham Palace. Fast forward a few years, and he was playing to a crowd of thousands at the palace for the Queen's Jubilee concert and receiving an MBE from Prince Charles for his contribution to music.

Ed's ballads on his various albums regularly make the top ten on charts around the world. His smash hit 'Thinking Out Loud' spent nineteen weeks at number 1 in the United Kingdom and was the first ever single to spend a year in the top 40. He won the Grammy award for Song of the Year for the ballad and continues to win Grammys, Brit Awards, People's Choice and MTV music awards.

Authenticity

Ed Sheeran comes across as genuine, compassionate and very likable. His easy personality shines and he seems natural and himself, whether he is taking a selfie in the street or being interviewed on television. People experience him as friendly and kind, so we are at ease and comfortable with who he is and his personal brand. He is loyal and demonstrates that by making time between gigs for his family, by posting photographs of family moments and events like his cousin's wedding in Ireland and writing tribute ballads for his grandparents. He is humble, modest, down to earth and someone many can relate to because he is personable. He not only looks and sounds authentic but is genuine in who he is when he communicates with his fans and the media. When I watched Sheeran on national television, sitting on a sofa with his legs up on the seat, chatting away with two journalists, I felt I was watching someone very present and comfortable in his own skin.

Sheeran is known for his messy hair and tattoos, and is happy in trainers and a hoodie. Thousands of younger fans will be able to relate to him simply because he wears casual clothing. His 60 brightly coloured tattoos, all of which tell a story of his life, show us that he is expressive, fun and unafraid to be himself. His image sends out a clear message that it's okay to be carefree with your appearance. Developing your personal brand through image matters as long as you stay true to yourself.

Having bright ginger hair meant Sheeran was bullied and teased like many redheaded children and teenagers. (As a redhead I can hold my hand up as someone who experienced nasty and cruel bullying while being labelled 'ginger nut'.) He's a role model for all the other freckled, pale skinned children with ginger hair who don't like standing out, and gives faith and strength to those at risk of being held back in their lives from succeeding because of hurtful events. In truth, Sheeran's beautiful red hair has helped him to visually stand out as a more memorable personal brand.

Watching Ed Sheeran in his suit, dancing like a pro in the 'Thinking Out Loud' video, you can't help but be deeply moved by his commanding presence and sincere look as he gazes into the eyes of his professional dancing partner. His bold decision to dance in this video rather than have a professional, and his commitment to master the choreography and technique paid off for Ed. This video made him sexy. He went from unconventional looking to stand-out sexy with every lift and move across the dance floor. I suspect it made every woman and even some men who watched it want to get up and dance with this tattooed redhead in a heartbeat!

And if you want to see more of Sheeran's authentic personal brand, watch 'Carpool Karaoke' online to be a part of Ed Sheeran's fun singalong with host and comedian James Corden.

Reputation

Warren Buffett's famous quote 'it takes twenty years to build a reputation and five minutes to ruin it' stands out for me. Ed Sheeran has been open about his past substance abuse and heavy drinking and has shared how fame affected him in a destructive way. He credits a childhood friend and girlfriend for bringing him back from the brink. Protecting his brand was made possible by his choice to take a year off work and throw away his smartphone. In an interview he talked about how he would wake up every morning to at least 50 messages, all with requests and questions, but not one ever asked him, 'How are you?' He went off-grid, did some travelling and deliberately chose to be only reachable via email. Protecting your reputation is as important as building and growing your personal brand and Ed Sheeran chose well for his wellbeing, music career and brand with his decision to retreat and regenerate.

Ed Sheeran has a reputation for being a very generous artist and in his early career he gave free concerts. He once even performed in the streets after a venue had closed. Word travels fast (just like your reputation), so this was a smart strategy even if it was unintentional and spontaneous. Giving away an experience for free builds loyalty, as people don't forget kind gestures. Based on my research and experience in business, it's essential to not always charge for your services if you want to strengthen your brand.

Our reputations are impacted by who we hang out with, who we work with, who we are seen with and who we collaborate with. Elton John has been supportive of Ed Sheeran as a singer, songwriter and musician and Ed has also teamed up with Beyoncé and Taylor Swift, both of whom have stellar careers and strong brand recognition. Often, aligning yourself with another respected and successful brand is hugely advantageous, as it allows for cross-pollination as well as sharing fans and followers, not to mention the creative genius that can occur during collaboration. When two brands merge, both get the benefits of the buzz that's created, so everyone wins.

Legacy

Ed Sheeran has shown young people how anything is possible if you keep on trying, be true to yourself and work hard. He left home when he was young, was broke and without a home but he stayed his course and never quit on his dream.

Ed Sheeran is unselfish and helps other people to succeed. His alignment with the surf-clothing brand Hoax in Suffolk shows his passion to support small businesses to grow; indeed, sales increased worldwide after he was seen on tour wearing their clothing. A strong personal brand can be a turning point for other brands if you have high status and a fine reputation. Making other people great says a lot about you as a human being.

Ed will be remembered not only for his music and productivity but for his ability to make a difference in the world to ordinary people, who have more enjoyment in their lives because they are elevated and uplifted by music and lyrics that touch their soul and move them to dance.

Brand drives business

Sheeran's concerts are often booked out as soon as the dates are announced, so to avoid disappointing his fans he tries to extend the shows so as many people as possible can attend. This demonstrates how faithful he is to his fans and sends a message of 'I am listening; I care; you matter'. A compassionate personal brand will draw in fans and drive business. We are only as good as our reputation and Sheeran's brand is built on trust. Trust drives business.

When he was getting started, Sheeran's marketing strategy was clever in that he released all his music for free. This built a loyal fan base and underlined how passionate he was about having his music heard. Making art was more important than making money. Today his music receives over 50 million Spotify streams a day and he is on the Forbes Top 100 celebrity list for his earnings — giving away the music early on was a high-risk strategy that definitely paid off.

What partly drives his business is regular, personal social media postings on YouTube, Twitter, Snapchat and Instagram. Well-planned online creative marketing is worth its weight in gold and Ed Sheeran is strategic in promoting his work. He sent out a teaser on Twitter of the single 'Thinking Out Loud' then posted a short clip on Snapchat. This led to hundreds of thousands of online shares, resulting in massive sales that broke records in the music scene.

Ed Sheeran goes the extra mile to look after people. Eleven-year-old Aimee Keogh appeared on *The Late Show* in Ireland a few years ago and was astonished at a surprise visit from Ed. He then offered to pay for her and her family to attend his concert in London. On another occasion, Kelly Dimmock received a genuine and loving video message from Ed after he saw a video of Kelly, suffering from terminal cancer, singing one of his songs with her son. It's these sincere responses from Sheeran that touch the public and grow a wider fan base. The more followers, the bigger the brand; and the bigger the brand, the more sales. Going out of your way to make someone happy is a positive move for your personal brand. People remember the small things and Ed Sheeran's humility, kindness and personal touch are drivers of his brand.

Ed Sheeran creates personal connections with his fans through using endearing childhood images of himself as a baby, schoolboy and young teen in his music videos. It helps fans and followers create an intimate relationship with him and makes us want more of his music in our lives, as we feel like we know and understand where his inspiration is coming from. Ed Sheeran is a 'feel-good tonic'. We buy from our hearts and Ed Sheeran's personal brand is all heart.

Brainstorming the Ed Sheeran brand

- His brand is authentic, uncomplicated, inspirational, zany, loveable and appealing to various age groups.

- He helps to put a smile on people's faces who are suffering, by reaching out to them.

- He shares his happiness by including his fans in his private life.

- He grows the confidence of others and gives people hope.

- He gives back to the community.

- He is unique, talented, generous, hardworking, kind and caring.

- He defines what it is to be human through his music and lyrics.

The Hemsley sisters, cooks and healthy eating gurus

66 We are part of a big movement that's talking about being healthy in yourself, being well in yourself, and that being the most powerful thing."

—Jasmine Hemsley[12]

Jasmine and Melissa Hemsley are British sisters who have built a powerful personal brand around their passion for cooking tasty, nutritious and healthy food while blogging and sharing their recipes online, offset by beautifully styled photos.

The birth of their business evolved naturally, after one of the sisters helped a friend create healthier meals. Jasmine then developed a food delivery service which Melissa joined her in running, catering to high-profile clients like fashion designer Vivienne Westwood. To add value, the Hemsley sisters created a blog and website, which attracted a book deal and then generated the creation of a television series, *Eating Well with Hemsley + Hemsley* for Britain's Channel 4. The cherry on top was opening an eatery at Selfridges in London, taking their brand to a whole different level of success.

Their joint personal brand on social media projects honesty, wellbeing and an emphasis on sustainability. They are also relatable and have a cool, contemporary style. If you are interested in organic, healthy and alternative foods, their recipes will catch your eye. And if you are a fan of ghee, the Hemsley recipes will broaden your cooking skills. I immediately became a follower when I saw that they often use bone broth, which is something I believe is incredibly good for you.

Authenticity

The sisters radiate confidence and come across as joyous about their work, but more importantly they project respect for each other and a close, genuine bond. Accessibility is the word that comes to mind; they are open and available to their customers. Their social media is saying, 'Have a conversation with us'. They share their personal lives with us as viewers, so we warm to them doing everyday activities.

Yes, they are both are very beautiful and young, and unfortunately good looks do sell, but it's not just about their image. Their recipes reflect their mission to help people cook healthy meals, even in the face of criticism from some health experts and nutritionists. It requires courage, conviction and long hours of hard slog learning not to take public criticism too personally. Every high-profile person will have negative press at some stage and people will not always like you. If they were my clients, I would encourage them to stay on the same course around brand-building and delivery, because both women have a unique presence, are authentic when talking and presenting, and are likeable.

Reputation

Their brand online shows them as ambitious, innovative, energetic, happy and in love with life. This makes them attractive to viewers, readers and audiences. The photos they use are simple but evocative, making their meals look earthy, organic and appetizing. They offer themselves and their recipes as fresh and original, and regularly ask their followers to try new flavours and combinations. Like most good food brands, they use delicious language and descriptive words.

The Hemsley sisters are known to be available and accessible and have achieved this through responding to posts and ongoing, sincere dialogue with their followers and clients. Not all media about the sisters is favourable, but, as I mentioned earlier, this will happen if you are constantly in the media. There is a lot of controversy around fads and food, so experts and journalists will challenge anyone operating in this sphere.

Legacy

As the Hemsley sisters are young and relatively new to the foodie scene, it's hard to predict what their lasting legacy might be. But I suspect they will be remembered for their savvy brand roll-out through social media and healthy living messages for their generation. Their speaking out about not dieting and wasting food will also be a lasting key reminder.

Also, never underestimate the power of siblings or families in general to build a really strong brand. This can add a tone of unity, loyalty and sometimes easy comedy and generally is a winning formula. Legacy is often built through partnering and pairing and, quite literally, can double your followers and success rate!

Personally, I also find it interesting how they have boldly etched a place in this overcrowded market of food and lifestyle, deflecting criticism that they're neither trained chefs nor nutritionists. It hasn't stopped them from passionately pursuing their goals, building a brand and shrugging off the 'tall poppy' tendency of some media. They, and their brand's trajectory, are women to watch.

Brand drives business

Both the Hemsley sisters are social media savvy and their regular blogging has caused their brand recognition and reputation to go viral. They walk the talk by blogging about meditation retreats they attend and sharing their holistic approach to living.

In a special Mother's Day video, the sisters and their Filipino mother cooked one of her favourite recipes, sinigang. I warmed to the sisters more when I saw the way they spoke to their mum with deep respect and love. Memorable videos humanize people while framing them as someone we know and have a relationship with. Bringing family into your social media posts is a smart strategy, as it's intimate and real. This scenario painted a picture of a mother who spent a lot of time in the kitchen cooking with her girls and evoked scenes from their childhood. It was obvious the girls share a special and happy relationship with their mum and this adds value to the family brand.

Brainstorming the Hemsley Sisters' brand

- Their brand is about healthy food that helps people think about their relationship with food.

- They help people by teaching them to cook healthy and sometimes untraditional foods.

- They share their recipes and their knowledge, and they promote sustainability.

- They grow people's awareness by selling organic, non-paraben products on their websites.

- Their brand is natural, friendly, energetic and happy and built around a passion for social media.

- They give back by teaching people how to eat food that is good for your gut and digestion.

- They are themselves.

2

How to define your personal brand

> ❝ Your beliefs become your thoughts. Your thoughts
> become your words. Your words become your actions.
> Your actions become your habits. Your habits become
> your values. Your values become your destiny.❞
>
> —*Mohandas K. (Mahatma) Gandhi, Indian activist*[1]

In a busy week, in a busy world we don't often pause to ask the questions, 'Who am I?' and 'What do I care about?' However, in answering these very big and existential questions, a template for defining your personal brand will emerge. And it emerges from honest and brave inquiry into what you believe and why because, as Gandhi suggested, beliefs rapidly manifest into becoming your thoughts, actions, habits, expressed values and ultimately your destiny.

When you can answer the apparently simple, but actually complex, question, 'Who am I?' you will have found the most authentic starting place, or first block, to construct your brand.

Here is my brand definition checklist to help you walk a path of discovery.

1. Identify your values

66 Living with integrity means behaving in ways that are in harmony with your personal values."

—*Barbara De Angelis, American author*[2]

Placing importance on living your values is a way to build your personal brand. There are many ways you can pinpoint what your values are. Making a list of your five most important values is a start. To do this, ask yourself, 'What do I stand for in life?' and take note of the words that roll off your tongue. Some of my answers to this question are loyalty, integrity, tolerance and social equity.

The list of values below might help get you started. Do of any of these resonate with you? Do any relate to how you lead your life? What do these words mean to you?

fairness	dignity	compassion
belonging	creativity	empathy
communication	freedom	joy
wisdom	generosity	love
acceptance	honesty	security
discipline	integrity	gratitude
tolerance	independence	recognition
hope	adventure	wealth
expression	justice	kindness

I was once asked by my boss, whom I respected enormously and was generally eager to please, to train the Prime Minister of my country. But the request didn't line up with my values. The policies and direction of this Prime Minister's government, combined with the fact that I had worked with his predecessor from the opposite side of politics, led me to say no to the request and, in so doing, to my boss. What I learnt from this experience is that confidence rests in conviction, and although my boss wasn't pleased I think his respect for me probably grew.

2. Prioritize your values

It's not always easy to identify the values that mean most to you, but it warrants serious reflection so that you can pay more focused attention to what really matters in life. Look at your weekly schedule on your computer, phone or diary. If you value health and put it at the top of your list but you work 70 hours a week, then you need to make some serious changes to align yourself with this value. If your family is a priority, count the hours you spend with your partner and children over a month in your calendar. It can be helpful at the end of each day to ask yourself, 'Did I live my values today?' If you didn't, you need to decide what you are willing to change in order to do so, and think about who you can seek support from to help you make changes.

When my darling frail and elderly mother was living alone in her small suburban flat, my priority after returning from living in London in 2012 was her safety and wellbeing. I lived with her periodically and cared for her until her death in August 2014. I placed my career and social engagements well after her needs. It never felt as if I was making a sacrifice because I was living one of my values: loyalty.

Exercise

When you live your values, there is satisfaction and joy in how you live your life and no place for regrets. What examples can you think of in your life where you've prioritized your values and times where you haven't? Note these down.

3. Align your values with your strengths

How do you match your values with your area of expertise? What are you good at? Are you doing what makes you happy? These are some of the questions I pose to clients when they are stuck in a rut with their job. You can have the best job in the world but you might not be passionate about it.

One of my clients, Luke, was a competent and talented lawyer working in a global top-five law firm, but he was miserable. We worked for many months on exploring his goals. Luke was masterful with food and he shared with me that he had wanted to go to cooking school for years, which is exactly what he eventually did. It was remarkable to witness his evolution. Luke had to recreate himself and take time out from the corporate world in order to work out what he really wanted.

Exercise

Make a list of five of your values and write down why each value is important to you. Some examples might include 'Integrity to me means honouring my word and keeping promises to myself and others' or 'Honesty to me means being true to myself and to others'. Have an honest conversation with yourself about each value. Ask yourself, 'What steps am I taking to follow this value?' If you find that you are not following your values as you would like, remember this quote by writer Anthony Robinson: 'Your life changes the moment you make a new, congruent and committed decision.'[3]

Now think of a time in your life when you made a brave new decision that changed your life. If, for example, the value of honesty is something you have decided to embrace, then perhaps you no longer cheat on your partner and decide to come clean by telling the truth about secrets you have kept to yourself.

Thinking about defining moments in your life can help you work out what your values are. You might, for example, have had an illness in the past and out of this experience you chose empathy or gratitude as important values to you. As another example, you might tell your boss, after some time, that your heart is no longer in the job, so you resign. The value of courage is something you will embrace.

It's a useful exercise.

4. Allow vulnerability and tell the truth about your weaknesses

66 Vulnerability is the birthplace of innovation, creativity and change."

—*Dr Brené Brown, research professor, University of Houston*[4]

A vital part of my work as a presentation coach is to encourage clients to be vulnerable. At the tender age of eighteen, I was told by a close friend that I was too vulnerable. I took this to mean that my fragility was a weakness. But it did not take me long to figure out that being vulnerable was a strength. Stay open when you are vulnerable; you never know what's around the corner. We learn lessons every day if we read the signs. As human beings, we are often more sincere and genuine when we are fragile.

Many of my clients dread the universal questions, 'What are your weaknesses?' or 'What are you not good at?' When helping clients rehearse for job interviews, I ask these standard questions over and over again until they feel at ease. We can spend a good 30 minutes just on this one question, as it can feel very uncomfortable. When you succinctly express or declare a weakness, it shows honesty and you get used to feeling vulnerable without going into a decline. The key is to not think of your weaknesses as a bad thing, but as an opportunity.

The most important thing I emphasize is to give an example of some area that you are working on to improve and never lie. For example, 'I am not 100 per cent confident when giving presentations but I have joined Toastmasters and am now feeling more confident when in team meetings.' It shows that you are actually addressing the problem. There are excellent articles and blogs on the internet from recruiters who can help prepare you for this question, so it always pays to do some research. The more you prepare, the easier it becomes to answer any confronting question.

5. Be self-compassionate

66 It's not your job to like me, it's mine."

—*Byron Katie, American author and speaker*[5]

Most of us need to learn how to be more self-loving. It's a concept that is foreign to many of my clients, but I continue to open conversations with them about the importance of self-compassion and how being kind to ourselves is at the core of building a strong personal brand. Facing what upsets us and makes us feel 'weak' actually starts us on the path to great courage and strength. If we cannot feel good about who we are and our behaviour, how can we motivate and inspire others? In forgiving ourselves we are acknowledging the truth of being human, which is that we are, all of us, imperfect.

From my experience and from observing clients, being compassionate and forgiving towards yourself builds your resilience, which in turn strengthens you as a human being and helps your personal brand.

What do self-compassion researchers say?

Harvard Medical School clinical psychology instructor, Christopher Germer, talks about recovering from failure. 'It's easier to bounce back from failure,' Germer says, 'when you are kind to yourself.'[6] In an interview with *The Huffington Post*, he added, 'Self-compassion is an important factor in emotional resilience. There's just a wide range of elements it enhances when it comes to emotional wellbeing.'[7]

Dr Kristen Neff, a self-compassion researcher and Associate Professor at the University of Texas, writes, 'The number one reason people give for why they aren't more self-compassionate is the fear that they will be too easy on themselves. Without constant self-criticism to spur myself on, people worry, won't I just skip work, eat three tubs of ice-cream and watch *Oprah* reruns all day?'[8] But Dr Neff urges us to consider whether self-criticism is really the great motivator it's cracked up to be. 'Research shows that self-critics are much more likely to be anxious and depressed — not exactly get-up-and-go mindsets. They also have lower self-efficacy beliefs [i.e. confidence in their abilities], which undermines their potential for success.'[9]

With her colleague, Christopher Germer, Dr Neff designed an eight-week mindfulness course about self-compassion in 2012. They published their results in *The Journal of Clinical Psychology*. The findings showed that at the end of the program the participants were more self-compassionate in their behaviour and they showed a decrease in stress, depression and anxiety.[10]

It's not easy to forgive yourself when you are the cause of any upset or unhappiness but, as Dr Neff says, 'Self-compassion comprises three elements: being kind to yourself when things are painful (self-kindness), accepting our pain and suffering without judgment (mindfulness) and recognizing that you are not alone in your suffering (common humanity).'[11]

We are not taught in school how to forgive ourselves, so we limp on into adulthood beating ourselves up and bungling our way through self-doubt, trying to learn the 'I forgive myself' ropes. This is easier said than done when you are blaming yourself for things that go wrong or you've made an error of judgment. Learning about self-compassion and having it be something real in your everyday life leads to a healthier personal brand. Over the past two decades, through reading and research, I have persisted with self-compassion practices and found that in time it gets easier to forgive myself when I stuff up. Making mistakes in a speech (like going blank) can sometimes dampen my spirit when walking off a business stage and these are the times I need to 'not beat myself up' and learn from my errors. Forgiving myself for not being perfect in my delivery is a regular disciplined practice. I ask myself 'Why did that happen?' and it usually comes down to a lack of rehearsal time or the fact that I did not make enough planning and writing time. Even saying out loud 'I forgive myself' is a start; speaking that phrase to a friend is also useful.

Comeback story: Martha Stewart

In 2004, Martha Stewart, who built an empire by marketing her own cooking, entertaining and decorating visions, spent five months in a federal US prison for obstructing an investigation into her sale of nearly 4000 shares in a biopharmaceutical company a few years earlier. On the day she was sentenced in a Manhattan court, Ms Stewart told her fans in an upbeat way outside the courthouse, 'I'll be back. I will be back. I'm used to all kinds of hard work, as you know, and I'm not afraid. I'm not afraid whatsoever.'

These were prophetic words from the lifestyle mogul. Although her company and reputation took a huge hit, she made the most of her jail time by befriending her fellow inmates, representing their interests to prison authorities and cooking for them. She even earned herself the affectionate jailhouse nickname of 'M. Diddy', which she embraced willingly.

Her resilience and humour helped her reclaim the respect of many who felt let down by her behaviour. She paid the punishment for the crime for which she was convicted and made an example of the idea that if you ride out bad times with grace, laughter and courage, you can set the compass for a fresh start. I have seen her appear on comic 'roasts' on TV and make funny quips about her time as a jailbird. This approach helps both re-build trust and foster re-branding opportunities, as it plants the seeds for forgiveness.

About a decade after her troubles, again in the witness stand for an unrelated matter, Stewart told the court room, 'I did my time! I stumbled in 2003. I had a terrible time personally. That could have taken down the company. It did not. That could have taken down the brand. It did not. They emerged whole and healthy.'[12]

It's hard to resist a rollicking comeback story and, more often than not, providing the circumstances are comparatively benign, redemption from ruin is available to us all.

Exercise

Read the questions below and write down your answer for each.

- When were you last compassionate towards yourself and how did this make you feel?
- When were you not compassionate towards yourself, and why not?

Service to others

❝ To give real service you must add something
which cannot be bought or measured with
money, and that is sincerity and integrity."
—Douglas Adams, English author and scriptwriter[13]

One way of finding out more about yourself is to serve others. The benefits of working without payment are endless and by giving of your time and talent you get back one thousand times more. Although volunteering means a commitment which will cost you time, giving without expecting anything back can be rewarding — and can help grow your brand. My voluntary work sitting on boards for not-for-profit organizations is my way of serving and sharing my expertise. Having a background in public relations means I have business networks I can tap into to raise sponsorship for fundraising. In a sense you are marketing your business and your skills by bringing your knowledge and contacts to the table for an organization. That's not why you are there but there's a bonus in everything you do by giving back, even if it's satisfaction that you helped a project get off the ground or a fundraiser generate a cash flow.

If you choose to sit on a not-for-profit board as a way to serve others, it's important to ask yourself two questions: 'Do my beliefs and values match this organization?' and 'Am I here because I want to serve and give away my time, skills and ideas, or am I wanting something in return?' This doesn't mean it's wrong or shameful if you use this experience as a stepping stone to be on a commercial board. But make sure you are an active board member, adding value and letting the other board members or trustees see who you really are and that you are fulfilling your role.

What is your purpose and your mission?

Finding your purpose is like discovering a treasure chest that has been forgotten on the ocean floor. If you know your purpose, others will be inspired to listen and follow you.

So what does this mean in practical terms? We all have unique talents but that isn't enough — we need to align this with our values to be able to unlock the chest where our purpose and mission resides. Sometimes others can see how our talents, re-utilized in different and original ways, can lead us to find our real purpose. Luckily, I had mentors who guided me away from the performing arts as an industry while encouraging me to use my skillset in business. This revealed my life's purpose and mission: to help people fully express themselves and shine on their own stage, especially in business.

Exercise

What are you good at in your private life? At work? In your community? Are you good with people, children or the elderly? Are you good with fixing things like computers? Are you creative with floral arrangements? Do you sing for a living or direct masterful plays? Are you able to manage a crisis, a city, a country?

Whatever you do, don't hold back from sharing your ideas or from describing how you can make a difference with your skills, knowledge and talents.

In business we use the phrase 'Unique selling point' to describe what you have that your competitors do not. This technical jargon sounds cold and for many of you it will perhaps be a meaningless and foreign phrase. But please hang in here with me, as it's relevant for you.

What is your unique selling point in your business? What sets you apart from others? What do you offer that others don't? Every business needs a unique selling point. I get asked this question often when I am pitching for new business or I have a conversation with a stranger. My response is that I bring a background of theatre to my work so I am creative in my thinking. And you will all have a different way of responding to this question. This question may help you to think about people living and working in your own community who offer something different and of value to you.

Amelia is a beauty therapist in the village where I live and her flourishing business is nestled in a tiny, peaceful studio in the back of the leafy garden of her home where she lives with her husband. Her clients are often on a waiting list to get an appointment because she charges half the price of most beauty spas in the neighbourhood and gives her clients exceptional customer service, which is personal, friendly and her clients, mostly women, leave with a smile on their faces. What she offers is not only good value for your money but the hideaway takes away her customers' stress.

Read through the following questions, then write an answer for each one. Take your time in considering your answers.

- What is your unique selling point?
- Why are you good at what you do?
- What are your core values?
- How can you best combine your values with what you are good at?
- What are your key goals?

Using your answers to these questions as a guideline, create your own purpose/mission statement. This is a valuable exercise and one I have done frequently in personal development programs. You will be more confident and secure when explaining your purpose if you are clear about your goals. Start your statement with the words, 'My purpose or mission is ...'

What does success mean to you?

> **"** I want to define success by redefining it. For me it isn't that solely mythical definition — glamour, allure, power of wealth, and the privilege from care. Any definition of success should be personal because it's so transitory. It's about shaping my own destiny."
>
> —*Anita Roddick, business executive, human rights*
> *activist and environmental campaigner*[14]

The meaning of success is different for everybody. In terms of shaping my personal brand, I've found it very useful to write down my definition of success.

My definition of success is much to do with how I treat other human beings in my work and private life. What matters to me is accepting people for who they are and never judging based on appearance, race, gender or religion. Loving unconditionally is also of great importance to me.

I have some clients who value money because they want to be able to live a lavish lifestyle. I have others who value money so that they can give their children things they never had, especially an education. Being successful to them means being wealthy. I have other clients who have left the corporate world to work for not-for-profit organizations because they want to give back to the community. So, at the top of their 'success' list is feeling satisfaction at making a difference to disadvantaged groups. I have a friend who designs jewellery and what motivated her to work from her home in London was the desire to be with her children. To her, success is defined by putting family first but also creativity and innovation. My personal assistant chose to work part-time for me while her mother was ill and needed extra care. For her, success is loyalty to family. All of these are different, but all are as important as each other.

Exercise

Write your definition of success. I encourage you to spend some time on this because it will result in helping you to be clear when defining your personal brand. It will also help you to determine your values. Have a conversation with a friend who also loves to banter with ideas around the meaning of success.

Your brand on the page

66 The privilege of a lifetime is being who you are."

—*Joseph Campbell, American mythologist*[15]

Once you've defined your personal brand, you need to transfer this information accurately into your current biography, résumé or curriculum vitae (CV). In my opinion, very few people think about their personality or their personal brand shining through from the page.

Often, people's stories and experiences are buried in endless academic and technical jargon. It's also a common mistake — and obvious — to excessively embellish.

Advertising tycoon, David Ogilvy, said, 'If you can't advertise yourself what hope do you have of advertising anything else.'[16] There's some truth in these wise words. I believe that most people struggle with promoting themselves in a CV. It can take weeks or sometimes months to perfect this essential assignment and many find it a gruelling and torturous task. In fact, I'm yet to meet anyone who enjoys it.

However, rather than thinking of it as a tedious and daunting job, try to see it as an opportunity to make yourself feel proud when you start to type your experience on the page. It's getting past that overwhelming moment and self-talk of, 'I can't do this'. You can, and someone will always help if you ask. If you haven't written your CV for years, start with bullet points that include dates and names of companies and roles, and then flesh it out. Work with a friend and ask them to interview you and ask questions to remind you of your accomplishments.

The best investment you can make is to hand over your life on the page to an experienced writer or wordsmith who has a track record of producing credible CVs. However, this is not always possible, especially if you are not earning or in-between jobs. The internet has thousands of good tips, so it's worthwhile doing some research. But whatever you do, always show your written words to someone for feedback, as a fresh pair of eyes can spot the tiny mistakes that we often miss in our own work. Employers or recruitment agencies can go to your LinkedIn page if they need more information, but you still need to be prepared to inject concentrated time in to getting your CV looking sharp.

What's the difference between a bio, a résumé and a CV? Sometimes there's confusion but everyone needs a credentials document at some stage of their life, even if you run your own business, like me, and are your own boss. My motto is 'always be ready to send it out'.

Bio

A bio, or biography, is a one-page document and is a summary to promote who you are and your accomplishments while highlighting major achievements like awards. There are debates and conflicting expert advice about whether a bio should be written in the first or third person and you can get confused when researching this subject on the internet. Both are tricky, as most of us do not like to be seen as bragging about our experience and don't want to come across as arrogant. I would advise you to choose whatever feels right for you. After all, the goal is to be authentic.

You want to capture the reader's attention as soon as they set eyes on your page, so you have to sell yourself in a way that's captivating. Your goal is to stand out from your competition.

My bio is requested by organizers of business conferences and events when I am a guest speaker and includes a photo. It's updated regularly so it's fresh, but the bones of the bio remain the same and I only flesh it out or make changes when I feel it needs it. If you are on the speaking circuit of any kind, a bio is essential in your personal branding toolkit. Corporates use staff bios to introduce a new employee and it paints a quick picture of the person's skills without lots of dates and detail.

Questions to ask yourself about your bio are:

- Is it interesting?
- Is it more informal than your CV?
- Is it on one page?
- Does it include a photo?

If you answer yes to these questions, you are ready to send it for review by a friend or colleague.

Résumés

Résumés are one- to two-page documents usually used to apply for a job. Think of a résumé as a way to market yourself on the page to secure that job interview you are longing for. The recruitment agency or employer is reading this, looking for your experience and the value you will add to a company.

Curriculum vitae

I read somewhere that 'a smart CV is like a smart advertising campaign'. This certainly rings true for me after many years of rewriting my CV. The older I get, the more challenging it becomes to edit it down so it doesn't read like a life biography.

In Latin, the phrase curriculum vitae means 'course of one's life'. A professional CV is intended to give the reader an accurate account and record of your background, often chronologically. It takes discipline to edit and chop pages, and it's a job most of us do not enjoy doing. So I recommend you show your CV to a trusted friend or colleague for feedback and ask for support so you can whip it into shape. Is your CV targeted at a job you want? Be very clear about what you want it to say and why. According to my research with recruiters, a CV should be no longer than three pages long, but most CV writers I speak to say it's also within the acceptable range to run four pages.

I have over ten different versions of my own CV depending on what I am using it for. All were rewritten by friends who are journalists or communications experts. Value your experience and take pride in the jobs you have done well over the years. Do not be shy about accomplishments. It took me years to mention some of my successes on paper because I didn't want to boast. Your experience and expertise need to tell an authentic story. What is it saying about you? Who are you being in this document? Would you hire you?

Free services

There are many free services to help you write and design a worthy and compelling curriculum vitae. Canva is a website that provides templates for all sorts of documents including CVs. Using websites like Canva will help you to design a beautiful looking document that represents you and your brand. If you follow the simple instructions on Canva you will get access to useful tools like over 130 fonts and a variety of over 50,000 templates and a range of colours. There are alternative services similar to Canva such as DesignBold, Snappa, Fotor and many more. A quick search online will reveal a plethora of options. There are also services tailored to specific needs such as marketing documents, social media images and website platforms.

First impressions on the page

In my research into potential employers looking at CVs, bios and résumés, I learnt that most hiring mangers take six seconds to read two pages. Think about that! What employers are looking for in the blink of an eye is that first good impression. Spelling mistakes and grammatical errors stand out, so avoid mistakes and looking unprofessional, otherwise you will end up in the rubbish bin. You want your personality and story to glow in a crowd of paper applications, so remove buzz words like 'passionate' and 'enthusiastic' and think about memorable content.

Commonly used clichés

Overusing clichés in your CV won't tell the reader who you really are. Imagine what it's like to read a pile of CVs all saying the same thing. Here are some clichéd words and phrases to avoid:

Hardworking	Highly motivated
Team player	Innovative forward thinker
Results driven	High-performing leader
Dynamic problem-solver	Thought leader

What do you replace these with? If the job description specifically asks for some of these as prerequisites, perhaps address them in your cover letter rather than in the CV itself. It's also very important to give evidence of how you achieved these things. This shows that you've really thought about what they are looking for and what you can offer.

Read competencies carefully

My client, Rose, who works in research for a university, was asked to assist in the hiring of a personal assistant for her boss. She shared how she was amazed to see that 50 per cent of the applicants did not have 'minute taking' in their CV. 'Did they not read the brief?' I asked. She had no idea, but she put applications in the rubbish bin if this skill was not included in the applicant's job experience. There's surely a lesson here: do not take anything for granted and read the job description carefully. Spell out your experience and make no assumptions, as the reader does not know you and cannot read your mind.

Having said that, what if you want to change jobs/industries or upskill in your role? Be sure to address this in the cover letter and be honest about your skillset while still being careful not to put yourself down.

What do the experts say?

Kristi Russo, American author and résumé writer, shared her tips in *The Guardian*. She advises clients to review their content and for every bullet point ask themselves the following:

- What value does it display?
- Why was this important?
- Who did this have an impact on?
- Did it save time, save money, increase productivity?
- When the next employer reads this, will they see it as a value you can bring to them?

'If it doesn't fit any of these categories, then it really doesn't need to be there,' says Kristi.[17]

Fresh Eyre Associate Allie Webber is the person I send all my clients to when they are reworking their CVs and the person I trust with my own CV. Allie says that 'everything you write in your CV should be accurate and able to be substantiated'. She maintains the best CVs follow her 'ABC rule' — accuracy, brevity and clarity. Take out the jargon and use plain language. Here are some more of Allie's tips.

- You need to tell the best story you can about your career and achievements, but it must be accurate. It's easy for a selection panel to cross check your 'claims to fame' online, so don't over-guild the lily.

- When writing your CV, think about how the information you provide answers the questions 'How much?', 'How many?' and 'When?'

- Anything to do with managing, projects, money or people is worth mentioning; well-chosen statistics are always your friends. Including this information will also help you answer the questions above.

- Use 'context boxes'. A common fault is that people often talk about an employer they've worked for, assuming everyone knows about them. We don't! So explain it in a context box. Here's an example: 'Rentz is an Australian family-owned and operated car, van, truck and trailer rental business with offices in Melbourne, Sydney, Suva and Auckland.'

'Be memorable, tell an accurate, authentic story about yourself, cut to the chase and get people with influence to recommend you,' says Allie.

3

Talent spotting your target market

" If you want to create messages that resonate with your audience, you need to know what they care about."

—*Nate Elliot, marketing technology advisor[1]*

What is a target audience? If you research this question you will find a standard generic answer like, 'A target audience is a group of people you want to connect with so they will buy what you are offering'. If you have knowledge about who you are selling to — that is, if you know your particular target market or audience — you can design and offer something extraordinary that changes people's lives for the better. So it's important to know your target market, and to understand who they are. You can then build a unique business that stands out and gets sensational reviews and attracts media attention. You can sow a seed and watch it grow. Then one day, with a sprinkling of luck to accompany the hard work and tenacity, you might be able to assert with pride, 'I did it. I am an international personal brand.'

Before I get into the detail of creation and identification, I want to focus on what is real, unique and organic about you and your product. That is your starting point. You have to love what you are doing, creating and taking to the market so much so that you are your own first audience/customer. Do you like what you are selling? What is it that grabs you?

Once you have passion and belief on your side, next comes the work of identifying who your market is. It's my intention to show you how to access your target audience by sharing some of my knowledge, stories, mistakes and client anecdotes. In turn, you can reflect on your own experiences and stories.

After giving birth to a new business and living and breathing our services, most of us are hungry and committed with great zeal to begin selling our offerings. Once you know who your audience is you can focus on smart and practical marketing strategies that will make your dreams become exciting realities. You can market your product to the appropriate audience.

Understanding why people need your goods or services encourages you to continually redesign and refine how you market yourself and keep up to speed in a digital world that is forever changing. Be very clear on why they are choosing you and the unique product you bring to the market. Always remember that you have something they need, so know your worth and tell your story.

Who are you reaching out to?

Who are you trying to reach in your community, your city or in your country? Do you want to position your personal brand on the world stage? If you don't know who your target audience is from the get-go, you may steer yourself in the wrong direction, wasting valuable time. You could get lost and confused in the dense forest of opportunities and ideas. You can be passionate about a specific audience you want to reach, but ask yourself and others you trust in the identifying stage if in fact your target is the right one. Be bold in your endeavour to get it right and do not give up if you stumble on the way. Making mistakes is the only way to learn.

When you are creating or reinventing your personal brand, you usually have someone in mind like a potential employer or the chief executive of your company. You are thinking of people who will want, need or desire what you have to offer. Does this sound like you? You may be hungry for a promotion or ready to start your own business and need a mentor to take you under their wing. Whoever your audience is, remember that building relationships comes first — well before the selling.

Matching your values

> 66 Integrity is choosing your thoughts and actions
> based on values rather than gain."
>
> —*Chris Karcher, American author and motivational speaker*[2]

This quote resonates within me and I am sure it will with you. One way of finding out who you intend to work with is to think about your personality and values while making sure you are not compromising your ethics, standards and what matters to you in life. (To remind yourself of your values and goals, revisit the exercises you completed in the previous chapter.) If integrity means a great deal to you then make sure you work with people who live and reflect this same value.

How do we know what values people hold in their hearts? That first time communicating with a potential client or employer is essential, so focus, ask questions and listen rather than talk too much. You have likely researched this individual online, spoken on the phone or exchanged emails and now it's your opportunity to get to know them in person. When it comes to integrity, take note of broken promises, such as a person not calling you back when they said they would. There's no need to judge (we all forget to honour our word from time to time) but be aware of small actions. This does not mean you should give up but do make notes of the communication along the way so you can see any patterns that emerge.

When you are in business meetings, listen for people's values and strengths rather than listening to 'fix' problems or to sell your services. By listening carefully to stories you will pick up on people's strengths. If one of your values is creativity, you are likely to bond easily with a new client who shares an anecdote when talking about encouraging staff or colleagues to be creative in their work. I have to stop myself problem-solving or starting to coach rather than listening when first meeting with a new business client. By paying careful attention, you get to know people's values and have more insights into that person's personal brand. Always look for what connects you with this person. You might both have children the same age, have elderly parents or live in the same neighbourhood, so be brave and find common ground by being yourself and building rapport before talking business.

Actors are taught about subtext in their theatre training and how to explore the meaning and emotion behind the spoken word. In business meetings, we need to tune into meaning and messages and what underlies a conversation, so we get to know what's really going on and what's authentic. It's simply a matter of being present when you are listening and not allowing your mind to sprout unnecessary thoughts, which distracts from fully engaging with this person. Building relationships is the key to growing your business and finding your target market.

Josie is a managing director of a global communications agency and new to her role after a promotion from senior account director. Over an early breakfast meeting, I asked her how the business and her new role was going in a tough, competitive market. We started talking about the company's values and she revealed how she had turned down a potential client who needed marketing for their chemical product. Josie is passionate about the environment and her team of consultants make a stand for environmental issues. It's never easy turning away business, especially if it's a large contract and you are being watched by your international boss to generate funds and build your brand.

Saying no and staying true to your personal and company values not only builds your professional reputation but can also open new doors and attract customers who respect your stance. Always trust your instinct and never be afraid to turn away something you do not believe in.

Who will buy you?

66 People don't buy what you do, they buy why you do it."

—Simon Sinek, author and marketing consultant[3]

A question to always have in your mind is 'who will help to increase my productivity?'

My challenge running a boutique company and with playing the role of a captain steering the ship, is to sometimes narrow my gaze and keep an eye on the horizon. My job is to be the visionary and keep on asking the question, 'Who will buy my products and training services?' Then I ask, 'Where do I want to sell our programs or my books? Where can we as a team make a difference?' Someone will always buy your product and all you have to do is keep on making an inquiry about the who and where. You know why you believe in your company or your offerings and you know your self-worth, so keep your focus on your target audience and you will continue to work with people who genuinely benefit from being in partnership with you. If you ever lose sight of your why or your purpose, go back to the drawing board, to your goals, your objectives and dreams, and remind yourself why you are pursuing your passion.

If your personal brand has a strong direction, you will always be sailing on course toward your target market. If you are happily employed in a company that you love, your target audience might not only be your boss but more senior partners, colleagues or influential managers who have your back. You might want a promotion and may need to find a strategy to demonstrate your skills in a whole new way so you stand out more. One way might be to increase your productivity; another way may be to sell a big idea that increases the company's profile and therefore gains your boss's attention and respect. Be very clear about who you are reaching out to and what strategies you are working on to reach the people who matter to you.

Why people follow you

Civil rights leader Martin Luther King Jr attracted millions of worldwide followers because of his ideas and philosophy about overcoming segregation and racial inequality for African–Americans. He wasn't selling a product; rather, he was promoting a powerful cause and movement which was so radically transformational that he received a Nobel Peace Prize in 1964 for his work around social injustice.

His target audience were African–Americans living in the United States, but his work touched oppressed communities all over the world. We can look at this man's legacy and learn from the power of one person's actions targeting a massive underprivileged audience oppressed by the scourge of discrimination and prejudice. Martin Luther King Jr was clear about his purpose and who he was fighting for.

In his famously crafted speech, 'I have a dream,' his words speak to two audiences. The first is African–Americans and the second is white Americans. You might have a variety of people in your target group who have different perspectives and agendas. Knowing your cause and beliefs means it's easier to find your target audience. Clarity around mission and purpose will help bring sharply into focus exactly who you are targeting.

Doing your homework and your research

66 Take all the courses in the curriculum. Do the research. Ask questions. Find someone doing what you are interested in! Be curious!"

—*Katherine Johnson, physicist*[4]

Doing your homework and your research is a valuable investment and an important way to spend your time. Researching a company online, asking friends or family, or approaching colleagues or former colleagues to ask if they know anyone at the company you are pitching to is a good way to start. The most important method of research I use is the phone. Often, I will call former colleagues or friends who might have information about a potential client that I can use. You're definitely at an advantage if you are filled with useful knowledge when pitching for work or generating new business.

One of the best online platforms for business networking is LinkedIn. It is the world's largest professional social network where you can grow your connections and job opportunities, as well as network in your field. It also provides a space for recommendations and testimonials from colleagues as well as an online résumé. A human resources manager heard about my work in the United Kingdom and went straight to my LinkedIn page to ask if I could work for her company when I returned to New Zealand during the holidays. This relationship continued for many, many years and today I am still working with this corporation. The following statistics for 2017 were documented in a post by Ready Contacts Marketing Data Insider:

- Total number of LinkedIn users: 467 million
- 71 per cent of professionals feel LinkedIn is a credible source for professional content

- As of March 2016, 27 per cent of LinkedIn users have between 500 and 999 first-degree connections.

If you haven't updated your LinkedIn profile for some time, or if you don't have a LinkedIn profile, put in the time and effort to represent yourself and your personal brand authentically on this very useful online tool.

Six degrees of separation

66 Old ways don't open new doors."

—Author unknown[5]

I am always amazed at how I manage to get in the back door by having a conversation with a friend in business. The idea of six degrees of separation is very true. I often get clients through a former colleague, family member or friend from years ago who has remembered me well from work done in the past. It's like a trail. You've left your footprints behind and they are tracking you down! Your next client could be sitting next to you on a bus, in a church, in a pub or at the school gate.

One of my favourite stories of six degrees of separation in my life took place in the United Kingdom. I met a high-end jeweller from New Zealand who I invited to my book launch. To my amazement, she and her business partner presented me with a beautiful necklace. The friendship developed, and she introduced me to her husband, who worked for one of the top banks in the world. This friendship then blossomed into my meeting the bank's chief executive, which led to this financial institution becoming one of my largest clients in the United Kingdom. Even to this day, he's still adding value to my business by referring me work in New Zealand, where we both now live.

Who is your competition for the same audience?

Embrace your competition. Don't bad-mouth them. My mantra is: thou shalt not think of them as thy enemy. Thou shalt think of thy competition as an opportunity. I was standing in the glistening marble foyer of one of my client's reception areas recently and unknown to me my competition was standing right next to me. My client smiled once we were alone and asked, 'Did you see who was standing next to you?' It was a reminder to remain positive. We'd just competed for a piece of work which he (my competitor) ended up winning because he'd worked with this client for many years and is good at what he does. I decided on that day to set up a meeting with this talented coach to brainstorm ways we could collaborate together. This is my preferred approach, because I believe there is enough work for everyone, and different personal brands can merge and make miracles for a client.

How to find your target audience

If you can't afford to hire a consultant or PR/marketing agency to help you identify and then market to your audience, here's a short exercise to get you started. Ask yourself the following questions. Then look at the table on page 85, where I've answered these questions using my own business as an example. Write your answers for your own business in the blank spaces in the table.

1. Get to know your business inside out. What are you offering? What are your strengths and weaknesses?

2. Why do you offer this product or service? What are your values and what drives you?

3. Who needs you? Identify clients or companies that might need your services. Be industry-specific.

4. Identify who the decision-maker/s might be in that company and research them.

Your product/ service	What do you offer?	Strengths and weaknesses	Why do you offer this product/ service?	What are your values and what drives you?	Who needs you?	Who are the decision-maker/s?
Training and coaching programs	• Presentation skills • Media training • Voice coaching • Image consultancy • Personal branding	**Strengths:** • Consistent powerful and positive testimonials • Long-term relationships with clients (over 20 years) • Talented associates with strengths and abilities in other fields, e.g. backgrounds in journalism, professional theatre and filming (trailblazers in their expertise) • Marketing background (public relations knowledge) • High-profile clients who have endorsed my products, e.g. prime minister and athlete • Published author (credibility) **Weaknesses:** • Lack of a sales team • Client too reliant on Maggie Eyre	To transform people and improve confidence in all areas including presenting and interview skills	Integrity, compassion, creativity, generosity, love, empathy, acceptance, fun, communication, confidence, growth, beauty, expression, trust, tolerance, recognition, responsibility, courage and kindness	• Corporates • Small businesses • Governments • Not-for-profits	• Human resources • Organizational development • CEOs • Private secretary • Executive assistant

Customer service

66 Strive not to be a success but rather to be of value."

—*Albert Einstein[6]*

Once you've started to identify your target audience, it's important to think about how you approach your clients and customers. We always remember how people treat us and we are left with an impression. Whether it be at the doctor, the dentist or the hairdresser, we pay money to be looked after and we have an expectation of good customer service. I often think 'target audience' is such a cold phrase. You need to remember that all we are actually talking about here is people. It's important to connect with your clients and build a caring and responsible relationship. It's all about good customer service, and the way to build this is to ask good questions so you can focus on their needs. The story below highlights the value of communication in customer service.

Alex, a young woman from Orpington, England, sits opposite me in my favourite hair salon in Tunbridge Wells, Kent. She introduces herself as my hairstylist with a genuine smile matching her vibrant purple lipstick. Her dark brown eyes peer at me through her colourful, edgy glasses. I immediately warm to her.

'What's your purpose?' she asks. I am taken aback, and I think, wow, this is good staff training. I have never had a hair stylist use the word 'purpose' in this context. Her inquiry made complete sense to me, and my reply is straightforward. 'I want to feel and look good when I get off the plane in two days' time in Milan.' After she blow-dries my hair, I ask Alex about the way she welcomed me and if she'd been trained to ask customers the question. But it was something she had never asked anyone before. I give her positive feedback and encourage her to use it again and again.

'What's your purpose?' is a smart and unique way to build a relationship with a new client. It certainly worked for me and we had quite an in-depth conversation about this phrase. It made me think about what I wanted and helped me to explain clearly what my objective was. I was able to share this with Alex so she could hear about the impact of her choice of words. I felt valued and taken seriously. On reflection, she'd cannily engaged in a sort of interview. She asked me many intelligent questions and her focus was making sure I got value for money.

Asking a client what their objectives are is something I do at the beginning of all my training sessions, but in a hair salon it felt unusual. However, it reminded me that words have an impact. Opening with a question can invite the other person to really concentrate and focus on their needs.

Integrity with your brand

Here's another feel-good customer service story about an experience I had in 2017 in Italy.

If I was a bracelet, I know exactly what I would be like. Apparently, so did two French sisters who in their seventies designed a spectacular chunky resin bracelet that became my favourite piece of jewellery. The different shades of browns with splashes of cream and olive green suited my pale skin and red hair, and the spots and stripes were funky and cool. Whenever I wore this eye-catching piece (and I wore it a lot because it became almost a signature part of my look) people would comment, prompting my musing that the bracelet was a lucky charm that made me unforgettable in meetings and presentations.

I found the piece on a sun-soaked summer's day at the Brera market in central Milan. First, I saw the bracelet, screaming at me 'pick me, pick me!' as if it were a puppy in a dog shelter imploring a prospective owner to peer through the cage. Then I saw the lovely elderly man with the gentle eyes and wavy grey hair, who stood by his market stand with grace and pride because, to him, his jewellery and fine original pieces were as good as the Crown Jewels. Alberto told my friend and me about his works, their back-stories and his life's work moving through different locations in northern Italy selling original designs. Even if I hadn't fallen in love with this bracelet I think I would have bought anything from this gracious artisan.

Back in New Zealand, after months of constant outings, the bracelet broke when the elastic threading all the pieces together snapped. I felt lost without 'her' on my arm, so I was on a mission, when I returned the next year to Milan, to track down Alberto and have him repair the bracelet and restore it to my wrist. My Italian friend, Giulia, and I set off one Sunday morning to see if Alberto and his stall would be where we'd found them a year before. We remembered he was only there one weekend a month, so we were uncertain of our chances. Sure enough, as we turned the corner we spotted him. Same stall. Same smile. Same gentle eyes.

We gasped as we ran towards him with the bracelet in my hand, me stumbling through my broken Italian with the story of the bracelet and its breaking and Giulia breathlessly filling in the gaps with her fluent Italian.

He looked so concerned and understanding and genuinely happy that he could put this piece back together. I asked him how much he would need to fix it. He almost looked offended. 'No! No!' he insisted. He would not take any money. This was his life's work and I as his customer deserved his full service. He then discreetly asked my friend for her address (where I was staying) and insisted he would deliver it within two days to her doorman.

Never in my life have I experienced such loyalty. Alberto was honourable and went out of his way to return my treasure, which not only made me happy but it generated many conversations about his integrity, so much so that here I am writing about him and his sincerity and inspired work ethic and practice.

Integrity and authenticity go hand in hand. Alberto, the gentleman with the huge, warm smile, will always be a warm memory when I think of

Milan. His generosity and integrity around his work and delivery will certainly motivate me to go back and buy more and send any visitors to the city to also find him.

How often do we make promises and not carry them through? How often do we taint our personal brand by not going out of our way to keep our word and make an effort to delight our clients? What do we need to do to in our actions to build more trust and loyalty?

Someone once said, 'Make integrity the corner stone of your personal brand'. Although a small businessman, Alberto is big on brand integrity and customer delivery. He fixed a problem, went out of his way to keep a customer happy and reminds us how personalized and committed action provides real service at its best. Grazie Alberto!

Saying no to clients

One of the biggest errors I made in my earlier days of running a business was to try to appeal to everyone. I couldn't fathom and didn't want to see the basic business fact that what I was selling wouldn't appeal to everyone. Because the truth in business is, not everyone is going to be seduced by your personal brand. Some clients may be drawn to you like bees to golden honey, but others could be turned off by your product, personality or what you stand for.

What does your perfect client look like?

66 Make a customer, not a sale."

—*Katherine Barchetti, founder of K. Barchetti Shops, Pittsburgh*[7]

In a company, I look for values that align with my business, for example integrity, authenticity, kindness and respect. I also look for what they do around social responsibility and how they give back to the community. I look to the top and do some research on whether the chief executive and the board actually live and breathe their values. Often when I coach just one person in a company, I'm surprised that they sometimes don't know the values the company stands for. There are other times when a client can reel off the values in their place of work.

Here are some useful questions for you to answer when deciding if a client is right for you:

- Is the client an ambassador for your personal brand?
- Does your client enrich you personally, professionally and financially?
- Is there synergy and common ground?
- Does your client share and introduce you to their own network at functions or events?

If the answer is no to some of these questions, how can you be more proactive and responsible to turn this around? For example:

- Do you make a clear request for an introduction?

- Do you ask to be on an invitation list to your client's events?
- Do you go out of your way to find new business for your clients?
- Do you endorse a client on social media and sing their praises?

My advice is that you become the perfect loyal customer to your clients and you will attract long-lasting business relationships that will grow your personal brand and your reputation. This has not only been my experience but something I practise with clients who keep on giving back.

Exercise

Describe your perfect client. What qualities and values do they have? In trying to answer this question, consider some of these prompts:

- Do you want to work with fun and inspiring people who are up to big things in their lives?
- Do you want to work with clients who have similar values?
- Do you want to be paid on time?
- Do you actively seek out clients who you aspire to and who grow you as a person?
- Do you market your services and products to your clients?

4

Digital presence: Your shop window

> **❝** If you make customers unhappy in the physical world, they might each tell six friends. If you make customers unhappy on the internet, they can each tell 6000 friends."
> —*Jeff Bezos, Amazon CEO*[1]

Walking past a visually stimulating shop window in any part of the world will stop me in my tracks, especially if it's bold, interesting and beautiful. Going online or into any digital space to learn more about someone's brand is no different for me. When I stumble across a powerful website with clever branding, I pause and make my way around the site eager to learn about this stranger or company. Peeking into their inner soul to understand what they have to offer generates immense curiosity in me and increases my appetite to know more. It is a moment between me (the browser) and them (the seller) in which a relationship is beginning and I am deciding, in a moment, if I want to leave or stay to get to know them.

This type of digital 'meet and greet' may be your very first encounter with a customer who could be in your life for a long time. If we want lasting relationships, we are on our best behaviour. We practise kindness and treat human beings with care. We try not to abuse, use, mislead or be disrespectful. If we apply the same rules in our digital partnerships, we will be more likely to have an honest and successful online and social media impact and presence.

To succeed in business these days, it is as imperative to be seen in the online world as it is in the offline. What word would you use to describe your digital presence? Is it something you are proud of? Does it reflect you and your business?

'Studies have shown that consumers encounter up to 20,000 brands every day, only twelve of which leave an impression,' writes Jeff Rum, an American digital strategist.[2] This suggests that the volume of people who are checking out your digital store front is more than you can imagine and probably can even quantify. In this chapter, it's my goal to help you learn how to transform your digital rendezvous with someone into more than a flirt; rather, into a lifelong relationship.

Be yourself

66 Engage, enlighten, encourage and especially just be yourself!
Social media is a community effort, everyone is an asset."

—*Susan Cooper, American social media strategist*[3]

I cannot stress enough how important it is to focus on your online and digital visibility in both shaping and communicating your brand. By managing your digital shop window and reputation you are firmly committing yourself to taking and owning control of your career. You are the whole package for people to see, praise, admire, learn from and look up to. Step confidently into being the personal brand you want to be, both face to face in the offline world and through careful and intelligent cultivation of your various platforms in the online world.

Pretending to be someone you are not is the biggest mistake anyone can make. People want the sincere you. I encourage you to try not to make mistakes that may damage your personal brand in any way. Many of us have embarrassing social media tales to tell and sharing them with people you trust will help you recover and move on quickly so as not to create a storyline that impedes your growth. By being yourself people will more easily forgive and forget, so do not dwell on your missteps or on what people think of you. If you make a blunder, apologize, front up and remember you are human! We burden ourselves with having to be impressive to get attention because we all want to please and be liked. This is normal and part of our conditioning, but you don't want to be called a fraud. Social media can be a curse and a triumph. Check in with yourself before you write or post anything online. Ask yourself, 'Am I being authentic? Is this the real me?'

As the earlier data from Jeff Rum suggests, your digital shop front means you are on display and being looked at from different corners of the globe, probably more than you know. The curious and the competition, your boss and your clients — everybody is watching you around the clock, including your future employer, the casual shopper and the serious buyer with a business objective. Sometimes, we think it's only our target market that is checking us out, but in my humble experience that's simply not true. There is a 360-degree panorama of people and entities from your past, present and future who are converging on your digital presence and watching as they weigh up if and when to connect.

Danger zone

66 Don't say anything online that you wouldn't want plastered on a billboard with your face on it."

—*Erin Bury, Canadian technology marketing expert*[4]

Celebrities and high-profile brand names can make one mistake and their brand is ruined overnight. The public and fans can be unforgiving. I made a fool of myself in an interview many years ago before I had sought media training, and when it was printed in the newspapers it felt as if every word and every comma was mocking me. To the readers it was probably fish and chip paper but to me it was months of squirming and embarrassment. Lucky for me, my less than stellar media moment can be forgotten because it was published in 'old media' and literally could be disposed of. These days, we don't get so lucky. Whatever is posted about you, the good and very bad, will stay in the electronic ether forever and every time someone peruses digital media to find out about you, the bad stuff will be on show for an electronic eternity.

Bad behaviour

Remember that what happens online stays online. So never hurt, bully or aggravate your audience. Before you post, consider if what you're about to say would be offensive to your mother or your boss. Your intention is to enhance your brand, not damage it. Even a harsh tone in your voice can be misinterpreted. You do not want people seeing you as arrogant or distant when you are not. Cyberbullying is cruel and dangerous. Trolls are insecure people who cause damage beyond cyberspace. I have seen lives destroyed and people sink into a deep, dark hole after being bullied and threatened. Stay safe and do not allow other's opinions to rattle your world.

Short window of attention

Our world has changed dramatically. We sit in restaurants, cafés and in meetings with our phones, flicking through a plethora of data, imagery, conversation, information or just plain 'noise' across the digital spectrum. In an instant, someone from anywhere in the world can be finding out if they want to work with you, hire you, and get to know you and what you have to offer.

According to the data, the average attention span of a Facebook user on a handset is 1.4 seconds.[5] This underscores how you haven't got long to grab attention, but you do have a huge market to grab attention from. You have access to a massive client pool through their fingertips. As social media specialists Ben Shaw and Jack Colchester wrote in an article, 'People's attention is out there, we just need to earn it, not buy it'.[6] So by taking the time to create or re-invent a user-friendly digital platform, you will arm yourself with the most strategic and efficient way of promoting your brand without spending huge sums on traditional advertising.

A word of caution, however. While standing out from your competition is important when trying to capitalize on the short window of attention you have, try to not become too caught up with this being your major goal. I think it's often best to gently ask yourself what's different and unique about what you offer and make that your starting point. In my case, what makes me unique is that I have a background in professional theatre and also public relations, so a theme of 'theatre in business' is a selling point. I have identified that a key part of my target audience is human resources managers and decision-makers in organizational development who hire experienced trainers. So I need my digital profile to speak to that audience and ensure that my website, platforms and social media presence projects the narrative and image of a strong woman who exudes confidence on stage at first glance.

Motivational speaker and marketing guru Simon Sinek uses his writing and talks to explore how to find the 'why' in your brand, suggesting that people don't buy 'what you do, they buy why you do it'. This is a very important concept to keep in mind as you promote your personal brand through the many digital options available to you. When you identify, embrace and live your 'why' you can authentically craft your digital presence, including your personal story and narrative, target messages for your audience and create engaging and memorable content.

Digital brands are personal stories

Most of the recent data collected around what makes people stop and pay attention to your brand when they are checking you out via a website and/or social media and digital platforms reveals that more than 70 per cent of people look for brand stories and not brand pitches. In the next chapter, 'The power of storytelling', we'll discuss how important it is to define your personal brand through unlocking your story and narrative. We'll also work on how to help you access the content and storylines that dwell within you and how this should combine with your values and commitment to future clients and employers.

The space in which most people will likely learn about your brand story is through one or more of your digital platforms. Apart from face-to-face contact, one of your digital platforms will most certainly be an equally important 'stage' for telling your story, so you need to think not only about the content but also about the colours, photos, font, design and all the stylistic elements that visually reflect and embody your brand. I personally love orange, which is the colour of my hair (I'm a redhead), and I often choose to wear orange, which has always perfectly complemented my pale skin tone. I will talk later about this in Chapter 8 , 'Styling your brand', but what's important to stress here is just how important telling your story thoughtfully and authentically is in the digital sphere. It could be the stuff of making your wildest dreams become real.

What does your photo say about you?

What photos come up when you google your name? Are they recent and really look like you? What year was the photo on your website or LinkedIn profile taken and is it up to date? If I see you in the street or in a meeting and you have beautiful silver-grey hair, why is it that your jet-black locks are still on my screen? Are you giving the wrong impression that in turn might give people reason to doubt you?

Does consistency matter? In a word, yes! Updating your digital presence is important to your personal brand. It's essential to water your plants and it's the same with your brand. Weeding out the old clutter to allow growth and regeneration should be high on your priority list.

Your picture suggests a thousand words so choose very carefully. Would you employ that person staring back at you with tired and sleepy eyes? Hello, anyone home? As the saying goes, eyes are the window to your soul — how can vacant eyes beckon us to hire or work with you? A photo where you look relaxed and friendly generates an air of confidence and likeability and encourages us to warm to you.

Use high-quality images on your website, in particular ones that reflect your personal brand. In my case, a professional photographer is not always available to take photos of me when I'm making speeches, so I ask the organizer to take photos on my phone for online use. Sometimes my personal assistant will come along and take them for me. Before I attend any event, I always ask if a photographer will be present, and if the organizer has hired one I make a habit of exchanging business cards with her/him, so I can easily access the photos taken.

It goes without saying that, especially when photos are being taken, dress your best and look sharp. Keep a file of the best photos that represent your brand so you can reuse them and be sure to create order on your desktop, so you can easily access them. I regret all the times I did not chase up photos or keep them logged easily on my own computer. Some favourite photos from work events in the past are now lost in the ether. Another useful idea is to keep a visual record of every job (paid or unpaid) that you do. It tells a story online and makes you look credible. Sharing yourself in real situations with a visual picture is sometimes more powerful than words.

At the beginning of writing this book I hired a web design company after looking at a client's stunning website. An instant professional relationship developed over a delicious latte with the owner, a brand guru. The company chose a photo of me for the home page that I would never in a thousand years have selected. It was taken at a book launch in 2016 at London's Hospital Club, a haven for creative people and my old stomping ground. Intrigued by their choice of the digital image of me wearing a glitzy brown sequin top, I realized how important it is to stand back and give permission to communication professionals to make decisions on your behalf. People who know my brand well pointed out how much they liked seeing a different side of me, not just the professional image of me in a suit. So take a note from me and think about the value of investing in a professional outfit, because a fresh pair of eyes can stand back and ask the tough questions we forget to ask ourselves, while providing a new perspective.

Do your research

Look at other people's online presence and when you are taken by something, seek details on who created it, why it was designed that way, how much it cost and any other question that serves your interests. If you decide to make a financial investment, hire a company who have an excellent track record and a gifted team of specialists, including quality copywriters. Smaller web companies hire in specialists who have an associate business relationship. Shop around and be clear about your budget, and be upfront about any need for payment options such as staggered repayments over a number of weeks or months. Most companies want repeat business from their clients so there's no need to be shy about making a request if you are on a limited budget. As a satisfied customer, you will spread the word and send new business their way.

Digital strategy

When I first set up my business, the biggest mistake I made was not being strategic. I didn't go immediately to experts and I tried to do it myself using Twitter, Facebook, and LinkedIn. I would have been better off handing it over to one person to manage. I also lacked the experience and passion to drive it. A digital strategy is simply having an action plan, and when you have a plan you have more confidence because you have steps to follow to achieve a long-term goal. The bonus of hiring an expert is that you are held accountable and work with this person or team and the job gets done. For some of you, you may be well and truly on your way and might not need any input, but for others you might need to know the key steps to take. I approached my strategist, Brya Page, who I trust and who assists in building my website, to give me some tips.

How do you create a digital strategy to reflect and grow your personal brand?

There are four key steps:

1. Define what it is that you want to achieve. Do you want to build a following on a platform such as Instagram, Facebook, Twitter? Or do you want to increase email subscriptions or sales? Be clear about what it is you want to achieve.

2. Define your target audience and who your future target market might be. Take note of the various platforms such as Twitter, LinkedIn, Facebook, Instagram and WeChat that reflect your target markets and are relevant to your brand, your products, and/or your services. For example, if your product is visibly appealing then Instagram is a good choice, or LinkedIn might be a better option to promote business-to-business services.

3. Build a content strategy around your target market's needs. Think about how you can add value for your audience. Establish set subject areas on your digital platform, for example tips, industry updates, topical and media-related articles, things happening in another industry that could be learnt from, podcasts, interviews, stories about people. Make sure that your brand is personable and positioned so it helps to create the perception of what the brand is, e.g. fun, rough, rugged or friendly.

There are three main points to remember:

- Ensure your online presence contains 30 per cent of what I like to call 'See it' — that is, things that amuse people, such as animals or something else upbeat and fun that's relevant to your industry or area of expertise.

- A whole 50 per cent of your online presence should constitute 'believe it' — content that paints a picture of you as an expert in your field.

- The final 20 per cent promotes your products and services; this is selling through your posts.

4. Create a 'content calendar'. Organize the content you will produce on a daily, weekly and monthly schedule. This will save you time and money and keep you on track. You can incorporate seasonal changes for topics; for example, engagement levels in winter are good for a wool brand whereas engagement levels from a cold drinks brand can come alive in the lead-up to summer. You can incorporate events like school holidays to ensure the most from your target market as well as special events, local events and weekly themes. Noting down the date, day and time your social media posts perform better, and what posts get the most engagement, is helpful.

Extra tips

1. Design and imagery are important to reflect your brand's personality. Is it fun, upbeat, approachable, sophisticated? Design, images and content are vital in portraying the right positioning, so it's important to get these right. Apps and programs can help to change the look and colour of images. Apply filters (such as VSCO filters) so that that all images used on your digital platform look consistent. Always try to have a

bank of edited photos and copy that you use. Do not use generic stock images, as they feel insincere.

Here are four free stock photo websites whose images are not your typical stock photos:

- Unsplash. This site has over 200,000 free high-resolution photos and is definitely worth a look.

- Pexels.com. Pexels has over 30,000 free stock photos and they add around 3000 new images each month.

- StockSnap.io. This site adds hundreds of new high-resolution images every week.

- Burst (by Shopify). Burst features a popular collections page, as well as a page for currently trending business ideas.

2. Influence marketing is about building relationships with people who can build relationships for you with audiences that your brand may not ordinarily reach. Connect with social media influencers and marketers if you can. Identity influencers for your market and assess them for relevance and reach. Be sure that their audience size and channels align with you and your services and brand. Share their content and thoughtful comments on their activities. If you're a product-based business, offer your services to them. Find out what you can do for them rather than what they can do for you.

3. Automation. Tools and platforms can help house and monitor all your social media posts, channels, analytics and feedback. Always link your website to social media channels and blogs.

Growing sales

66 Social media will help you build up loyalty of your current customers to the point that they will willingly, and for free, tell others about you."

—*Bonnie Sainsbury, Canadian digital business strategist*[7]

For the third edition of my book *Speak Easy*, I introduced book sales online through my website for the first time. In one month, I sold around 1000 books, which was a first. My book sales also increased in an hour after I was interviewed for four minutes on a breakfast television show. Stuffing the envelopes, licking the stamps and sending my book out in to the world was a pleasure!

Make sure your digital shop is set up if you want to sell books or products. I missed out on fourteen years of direct book sales simply because I was not prepared. I now direct people to Amazon and to my website and it is a thrill when I see how many sales I've made in a year. All effort is rewarded.

What do people think of you?

> ❝ People want to do business with you because you
> help them get what they want. They don't do business
> with you to help you get what you want."
> —*Don Crowther, social media marketing and online marketing expert*[8]

Ask colleagues, friends and family what they think of your online presence. Be specific and ask them to look at all your accounts, including Instagram, Snapchat, WeChat, LinkedIn, Facebook and any other social media platform you use. Take on board any criticism and use this advice to make some changes. Ask yourself and others, 'Is my personal brand credible in the market?' Email people you trust so you have a record.

Another good question to ask is: 'Is there consistency across all online channels?' Clients ask me to provide feedback, which I do as part of my service; they don't just want glowing reviews, but rather, an honest and constructive critique to make them stronger and better in their respective market. It's best to tell the truth and be constructive when asked your opinion and be sure to allow yourself to listen to the feedback others have for you.

Online tips

Here are some final tips to help you get the most from the most popular digital platforms in boosting your personal brand.

Twitter

> 66 Everybody starts out with nobody listening to them and nobody to listen to. How and who you add determines what Twitter will become for you."
>
> —*Laura Filton, co-author of* Twitter for Dummies[9]

When coaching in London, I relied on Twitter to spread the word and fill my weekly classes for people suffering from social anxiety; without it, there would not have been a full class. All credit went to the class organizer, who was a whizz at social media.

Tweeting rules

Twitter is a very effective platform through which you can communicate with your potential market in short 280-character messages. Here are some tips to help you get the most from it. Think of Twitter as a way to network with people you do not know; it's also a valuable way to let other brands all around the world know what you do.

- Devote some time every day to Twitter.

- Make sure to write an exciting bio so more people will follow you.

- Follow individuals and companies you are interested in to grow your network (try to follow at least two people a day to keep your profile active).

- Don't just promote yourself — retweet other tweets, and endorse other events and ideas.

- Be creative and add your own text.

- Tweet about daily trends and topics to gain exposure — but make sure to adapt them to suit your brand and network.

- Engage with those who mention you, but ignore any trolls.

- Use photos and images to add visual interest to your tweets.

- Be authentic in your tweets.

Tweeting disasters

As with all digital platforms, there are some pitfalls with Twitter. Here are the main ones to avoid:

- not making your tweets personable and creative

- not building strong relationships

- spreading rumours and false information

- constantly tweeting to promote your brand or products

- spelling and grammar errors

- insulting others — think before you type

- complaining about your job, boss, company, etc.

- not building relationships with supporters of your brand

- thinking negatively when tweeting — be positive.

LinkedIn

> " LinkedIn is a channel to increase, not a tool to replace, your networking efforts, and it is an excellent vehicle to facilitate some facets of your marketing and business strategies."
>
> —*Viveka von Rosen, LinkedIn expert and author*[10]

- Include a warm, friendly photograph.

- Make sure all the information you present on your LinkedIn profile is up to date. This includes not only your employment record but also any skills, training and experience.

- Use your LinkedIn profile as an online résumé that is easily accessible for potential employers or business contacts.

Setting up a good website

- Hire the right people to help you achieve a professional-looking website, including design and copywriting experts.

- Be careful when choosing images for your website and trust the experts.

- Make it user-friendly and easy to navigate.

Facebook

- Think about your online reputation — the photos you use, the groups you follow and the posts you make.

- Use Facebook to grow your network even wider. Make sure your posts are relevant to your business or industry; and make sure your copy is clear and succinct. Boost your posts to reach more people by investing a small budget so you get more comments. Invite your users to like your page.

- Post relevant, engaging and helpful content and link it to your website or blog.

E-newsletters

Sending a regular e-newsletter to your customers or target market can be an effective way to keep them up-to-date with your business or services.

- As a key marketing tool, use this to promote your brand and your services to those who follow you.

- An e-newsletter can be a great avenue to offer something for free, such as top tips.

- Make the newsletter content relevant to those you are targeting.

- Link it to your online website or blog to offer the readers more.

Blogging

- Like an e-newsletter, use blogging as a way to promote your brand and services.

- Write clearly and make sure the content aligns with your services.

- Use images that will capture the reader's attention, and make the messages short and to the point.

5

The power of storytelling

" Great stories happen to those who can tell them."

—*Ira Glass, presenter of* This American Life[1]

We all have stories. The very fact that we are alive and creating work, relationships, breakthroughs, failures and memories means we are 'writing' our life story every single moment in every day.

Stories are transformative. A story told well has the power to transform the way we perceive our lives and the way others perceive us. Great narratives create a lens through which we see the world and through which others see us. This is a very powerful idea to understand and, once embraced and incorporated in your life and business, huge breakthroughs with big outcomes await.

But the art is to harness those stories and then learn how to tell them in a way that is moving, compelling and animated while reflecting a truthful account of events. A story has a beginning, a middle and an end. A story has tone and colour. A story paints vivid mental pictures and inspires others to access their own memories and emotions, both joyous and painful.

Your story is a personal account of what it means to be human. It is about where you came from, what happened to you and why it happened. It tells of the child, the adolescent and the adult who made choices based upon talent, insecurity or sometimes a combination of both. You are the central character in your story and as the author no one knows you, your motivations, your values and your plot lines better than you.

I strongly believe that the more you are aware of the power that lies in the authorship of your life's narrative, the more you will fully embrace the privilege of being alive and ask yourself daily, 'What am I going to do with today? What am I doing with my life?' Our lives are scattered with hurdles, challenges and falls but great stories are often built upon the embracing of personal courage to get up, dust yourself off and dare to boldly live, love and work once again.

Telling your story helps your brand

66 Brand stories should be told with the brand persona
and the writer's personality at centre stage."

—*Susan Gurelius, marketing veteran*[2]

There are real rewards in being able to harness and tell your personal story when building your brand. In fact, the two should be considered sides of the same coin: your story and its narrative is the story and narrative of your brand.

Telling your personal story in a compelling fashion will help:

- you/your brand to stand out
- clients to know more about who you are (brand recognition)
- build relationships
- cultivate trust
- clients to listen, engage and remember you
- your mission and message to be clearly understood
- people to have an emotional connection with you.

Experience has taught me that you stand out more if 'the real you' is present in your storytelling. If we tell relevant and engaging stories and use colourful examples, our customers or clients know who we are and are more likely to believe us. Stories connect us to people. They make us feel emotion — so much so that we identify with parts of a compelling story. That's why talented playwrights haunt, move, anger and inspire an audience.

In one of my workshops, called 'Creating Presence', I encourage clients to find the stories within themselves and tell them. (On pages 117–120 is the exercise I use to help people discover their personal brand.) Often workshop participants are moved to tears, because when the storyteller shows his/her vulnerability they are transported inside the experience and touched at the core of their being.

Telling stories means you have a greater chance of being memorable and standing out as a strong brand, so it's essential to personalize your narrative. In doing this, people are more likely to want to build a relationship and enter into your inner world, because they feel closer to you and trust you.

Examples

Think about people who successfully combine their personal stories and brands. Examine how and why their story and brand captures your attention and imagination.

An example for me is the British singer Adele. She has sold over 40 million albums, won fifteen Grammy awards, and with soulful voice sings the poetry she has written about her life stories and heartbreaks. When you listen to her work and watch or read an interview with her, you are left in no doubt about who she is. Adele is honest and authentic about her storyline — how she grew up without a father and was raised by a young single mother without money and means, how she was discovered and the relationships that broke her heart but inspired her to pen many of her hits. Despite scrutiny about her looks and pressure from the media to lose weight, Adele refuses to conform to a stereotypical look, quipping, 'I don't make music for eyes, I make music for ears'.[3] She also is honest about the acute stage fright and anxiety attacks she suffers from, which sometimes cause her to vomit.

When I think about Adele, it is hard for me to separate the woman, her story, the talent and the successful business she has built. She has indeed nailed how telling a story honestly and compellingly becomes the narrative for your brand.

Exercise

66 You are the storyteller of your own life, and you can create your own legend, or not."
—*Isabel Allende, Chilean novelist*[4]

Here is an exercise I use in my courses and with my personal clients. It is a pathway to discovering your own personal story that will underscore who you are as a brand. Use this outline to kickstart the writing of your own story, writing down some information for each of the points below.

'I'm [name].'

- If there's something interesting about your name or it relates to your business, tell us about that.

- Always use your last name.
- 'I come from [your home town, city, country].'
- If you come from a small town, tell people where it is.
- Is it famous or infamous for something?
- Is there something funny you can say about it?
- 'I'm currently the [name your business and discuss what you do].'
- Make a note if you were nominated for an award — example, 'I am the only woman studying an engineering degree in my class at university.'
- List any national or international titles you hold, for example, 'I was nominated Woman of the Year for Business in Austin, Texas.'
- Tell people your ranking in your role or business if appropriate. For example, 'I am the first African–American to be CEO' or 'I'm the second woman to head the company'.

'Now I want to share the story about how I got into [name your business role].'

Start at the beginning. Talk about when you got into [your business] and why, making note of the following:

- What are your most vivid memories of your beginnings? Paint a picture of that time, the day, the moment.
- What happened after that to get you where you are today? (Keep this interesting and brief.)
- Describe your first promotion, accolade or recognition by your peers in your industry.

Inspiration

This is about the people who've helped you get to where you are today.

- I suggest you think of up to three people, such as your coach, a family member, someone in the industry you work in, a role model or hero or heroine.
- Think about how you would describe your greatest sponsor or mentor. What difference did they make to you and why did they believe in you?

Three things I've learnt along the way

What are your key lessons? Some examples might be:

- Never give up.
- Stay true to your values.
- Always back yourself.
- Ask for help.
- Be patient.
- Set goals and stick to them.

What's the most important thing you have understood?

Some examples might be:

- It needs to be fun. For me, in my personal and professional life, there has to be enjoyment. Every experience in my private and working life has to have an element of fun, which means that people around me are experiencing some form of joy, and that makes life worthwhile.

- You have to love it enough to get out of bed on a cold winter morning for it. We can find pleasure in everything we do, with a positive attitude. If I feel satisfied with everything I do in life, people around me will benefit. If you have fun, you enjoy yourself and so do others around you. As a teacher, I have learnt that when people are having fun, they listen and learn more.

Questions to delve deeper

- What 'hurt' you the most on your learning curve, or affected you most deeply? Note some ways in which this affected you; did it, for example, make you stronger or more grateful?
- What are your deepest values and how do you embody them?
- Think about your personal ethics. What issues make you want to take to the streets and protest? What will you stand for? What won't you stand for?

Now that you have written your story using these headings you can insert this page on your website or memorize and use it in a speech or presentation to inspire your viewers or any audience. Another way of using this content is to make a short video telling your story.

Taking off your armour

66 There can be no risk without vulnerability."

—M. Scott Peck, American psychologist[5]

I have talked a lot about authenticity when building a personal brand. But what does that really mean? And how do you foster it? The very nature of being authentic is to know yourself intimately because you have peered into the darkest spaces of your being as well as basked in the light. So ask yourself with great honesty: do you know yourself? Have you done whatever it takes to stare yourself down in the mirror and taken a hard, long look even at the stuff you'd like to pretend doesn't exist?

I am not a psychologist or psychoanalyst and I have no formal training in mind science. But I am a businesswoman of 30 years' standing who has meticulously built a brand based on who I am and what I believe, and by upholding the values that reflect my mission in the world. To do this, I have chosen to do a lot of work on myself and remain in constant conversation with every part of my past and present from which my storylines are drawn. I have coached and mentored people who have bravely allowed me to meet their skeletons in the closet, the very ones they have gone to great lengths to hide. But they had the courage to seek help because they knew that their apparently 'dirty laundry' was holding them back and causing great personal and professional pain and loss.

Building a personal brand and a business is like anything in this life. You will be rewarded for your strengths and the hard work and creative solutions you animate. But the shadows in your life — the areas, events or behaviours of the past that haunt you even as you build sturdy barricades so nobody will see them — will manifest and be the very things that hold you back, minimize your successes and accentuate your failures.

So hear me out. What is it about you that you are trying to hide? What needs work? And what are you prepared to do about it? Can you receive critical feedback without getting defensive and fortifying your barricades? When someone says something you don't like, do their words pierce like bullets and send you running for your shield, or do you disarm, make yourself vulnerable and accept the incoming 'fire' because it will make you stronger? We are all imperfect creatures, so there will be an area that you are either subtly or very obviously avoiding. Are you courageous enough to face yourself? My hope is that you are, otherwise it will be virtually impossible to truly realize your full potential and be authentic in your brand and your life.

> 66 When we were children, we used to think that when we were grown up, we would no longer be vulnerable. But to grow up is to accept vulnerability. To be alive is to be vulnerable."
> —Madeleine L'Engle, American novelist[6]

I am proud to admit that I am a graduate of many training courses and years of therapy, and I have spent decades engaged in personally researching and studying new technologies around personal development and mind sciences. This commitment shows up every day and in every way, but above all it has taught me to embrace my vulnerability. I have read and listened with delight to social scientist Brené Brown's work on shame and vulnerability. In her 2010 book *The Gifts of Imperfection*, she described cultivating authenticity as 'letting go of what people think'. In her 2012 bestselling treatise *Daring Greatly*, she asserted, 'It starts to make sense that we dismiss vulnerability as weakness only when we realize that we've confused feeling with failing and emotions with liabilities.' She goes on to explain that if we want to reconnect with our vulnerability and uncover purpose in our lives, we must engage with that vulnerability despite the sometimes uncomfortable emotions this brings.

Even now, as I run my business and train people around the world to step into their own potential and harness their brand, I still check in with my motivational coach who helps me examine the things I might not be able to see and overcome anything that might be holding me back from performing at my optimum level and continuing to reach higher. He also helps me get real and honest and in that spacious and honest environment I can recalibrate and recreate.

I am a huge believer in supervisors; even when you are performing at your peak, and also when you are falling short, you cannot see what you cannot see. You might need a second pair of eyes and a trusted observer to help you break through. I know this has always been my strength and something I continue to advocate for all my clients. Here are a few golden principles my motivation coach has passed on to me.

- In the moments when I am being true to myself I know I am being authentic. Authenticity is a personality trait I aspire to with a passion. It means I can be trusted.

- Over the decades I have claimed a cluster of values that remind me of who I really am. I do my best to be honest, reliable, consistent, flexible, enduring and a few other critical values.

- I have been fortunate to have focused mentors who have skilfully alerted me to who I really am. They have listened to me and coached me into being real and accurately self-aware. (That's been painful at times!)

- The Italians have a beautiful saying: 'The truth always bubbles up to the surface'. I love that.

- In my journey to be authentic I discovered that I can't be authentic without being a good listener at the same time. A deep, practised listener. Listening is the best path to the truth. It's no highway, but rather a rocky road. That's what my mentors are for.

Getting your act together

We all have different ways of coping and adopting strategies to improve our lives. I for one have experimented with a variety of master plans. To discover in my twenties that I had a short attention span was no surprise. I was a hyperactive child and teenager with endless energy, and I lacked focus. The patient Roman Catholic nuns who educated me at school were always trying to find a new way to rein me in. I am forever grateful to these wise and intelligent women who were my mentors, guides and advisors. My school reports frowned on me year after year, shouting from the page, 'Margaret needs to focus and concentrate more'. This was true but at the time I resented this phrase that became so familiar and like a broken record. My monkey mind still has its place in my life and challenges close friends and confidants. My preference is to experience and describe this as creativity; however, I consciously need to make an effort to be more present.

Meditation adds the most value to my personal and professional life. It stills my mind and helps me to be more centred and calm. I have used meditation techniques and attended courses for 40 years. I notice a big difference when I do not attend regular meditation classes — I do not manage stress as well. Studies show that meditation not only lowers your blood pressure, but it helps you to live a more authentic life. My clients who meditate are stronger and more in control of their minds in their business roles. They rarely express anger and are clearer in their decision-making. This has also been my experience and we sometimes run a short meditation in our presentation courses as a way to relax and manage the nerves.

Pilates classes have improved my wellbeing over the years. Having a trainer or a coach is something I need, as I lack the discipline to go it alone. For me, Pilates is like a moving mediation because it involves the breath. There are inexpensive classes all over the world, so investigate this if you are interested and find a teacher you feel comfortable with. If you stick at it, you get toned and feel healthier as a result. It's gentle and easy to do even if you are unfit or have an injury.

Many of Fresh Eyre's clients attend meditation and mindfulness classes to improve memory and relax the mind and body. Part of my job is to steer clients in the right direction so they can trial courses and find a teacher that suits them. My belief is that we come across as more authentic, sincere and grounded when we are calm and happy. Here are a few strategies for you to consider:

- **Meditation.** Reduces stress and anxiety, improves concentration, calms the mind and increases inner peace. When you meditate you learn to be a more compassionate human being toward yourself and others.

- **Mindfulness.** Improves positive mental health, improves work–life balance and teaches you to pay attention to the present moment. When you are mindful you are more aware of your presence.

- **Group training.** Ask people you trust about the courses they recommend in areas you're interested in. Do you want a public speaking course to help you be more confident and authentic? Do you want a personal development, non-religious or a more spiritual program to help you become more aware and open? When participating in interactive group training you realize you are not alone and learn from listening to others share their stories. It's also a great way to network and increase your personal and business contacts.

- **Journalling.** This practice increases self-awareness, is an outlet for expressing emotions and is therapeutic. Writing down your thoughts helps you to better understand yourself, and seeing your words and ideas on the page enables you to articulate them more clearly to others.

- **Therapy.** Therapy can provide you with practical strategies to manage life's challenges and overcome past or present trauma. Find a qualified specialist in a particular field by asking your GP or a trusted friend for recommendations. Do you want to see a clinical psychologist, psychotherapist, counsellor or a psychiatrist? Do your homework before you invest your money. Some counselling services are subsidised by your government, so tap into community health clinics and resource centres. You can also search online for the specific type of counsellor you need, using words and phrases like relationship counsellor, anxiety, depression, low self-esteem. If English is not your mother tongue seek out a counsellor who speaks your language.

- **Motivational coaching.** This kind of coaching helps you work on your goals and be accountable, inspires you to achieve the big dreams you might have given up on, keeps you positive and gives you coping techniques to problem-solve. Motivational coaches are trained strategists who help you recognize your strengths and set measurable goals. Some names include life, executive or performance coach.

- **NLP.** Neuro-linguistic programming improves communication skills, reduces resistance to change, helps you learn about how people think and provides a series of tools that teach you about 'how' to achieve results. It is excellent for business leaders, managers, team leaders and sales directors.

No thanks! Not for me!

You might have read this chapter with diffidence or even a sneer, and concluded that doing some work on yourself and taking a look at what is really going on in your interior world is unnecessary and not for you. And you would not be alone. But here's the thing: if we let our shadows eclipse our light, if we carry around the burden of suitcases full of dirty laundry, blame others for our misfortunes and pain and not claim our true vulnerable self; it's almost a universal truth that this will, pardon my language, bite you on the butt. And it will bite in your personal life and your professional life.

Being present to what is really going on in you and acknowledging the full range of your inner world is likely to shift something in how you show up in your personal and professional relationships. Doing personal work can often lead to huge lightbulbs going off and whole new creative chapters being written. I have seen it happen because I have seen it happen in me. I'm also a cheerleader for those who have the audacious courage to face their vulnerabilities and dare to be truly authentic in their life and work. These are people we want to know, hire, shake hands with, do business with, buy products from, have on our team, promote and vote for.

I will never forget the day after Hillary Clinton lost the 2016 US presidential election and took to the stage to make her postponed concession speech. Facing a stunned world, arguably the most famous politician on the planet, with a brand spanning over 30 years in public life, she found the voice to console her diehard supporters, comfort those who voted for her while fearing her opponent and also attempt to reassure a world that hadn't expected the result. The Hillary who took that stage was an entirely different person from the politician who had campaigned for and expected victory 24 hours prior. Her tone was sincere, her voice revealed her emotion and the pain of defeat, she wore her vulnerability and she felt and sounded wholly human, exposed and real. Since that time, in any of the interviews I have seen or heard from her, especially around the publicity for her book, *What Happened*, she appears quite transformed from the 'Running for President' brand she inhabited in 2016. I see her warmth, wit and humour more than she ever allowed us to see on the campaign trail. She is still fierce and rigorously intelligent, but I am left feeling as if I know this woman. I know this mother and grandmother. And I know this former senator, secretary of state, first lady and first woman to secure a party nomination to run for President of the United States. I wonder sometimes if we had seen this Hillary, would the result of the 2016 presidential election have been different?

People vote for, do business with and enter into relationships with those they perceive as being authentic. And to be truly authentic takes as much courage as you can muster and will set you apart from the pack.

6

Presentation skills to build your brand

66 The biggest thing holding people back from building a great personal brand is waiting until things are perfect."

—Lauren Clement, award-winning personal branding specialist[1]

Why do we need to care about how we present? Why are presentation skills so critical to improving a personal brand? In this chapter, I share my extensive knowledge about presentation skills to help you be more confident on any stage or in the digital world. I like to draw upon my experiences in the professional theatre when talking about having presence.

Confidence comes and goes in our lives depending on fleeting circumstances. We may have a perfectly crafted script but if we are not expressive and engaging we will send our audience to sleep or force them to turn the digital page without any hesitation.

Your presentation skills are judged every day and can determine the next stage in your career, so why would you not commit to mastering this craft? In the 'Creating Presence' workshops that my team and I stage around the world, we teach managers and business leaders how to present from a place of authenticity and give each person different feedback based on what they need.

Communication

If you study the art of communication, you will become a more eloquent storyteller and you will improve your interpersonal skills. As human beings, we are scared to make mistakes and want desperately to be liked. We do not grow up celebrating our slip-ups; instead, we try to appear unfailingly professional and capable.

However, our inner critic frequently jumps out in front of us to spook and sabotage our wellbeing. It's a bit like an out-of-control tornado of thoughts running havoc in our minds. When I was younger, I was extremely self-critical of my performances when presenting, especially when watching a video of myself making a speech or playing back a previous interview. My advice to you is, do not try to be perfect. If you do you will never start taking small steps, let alone giant leaps. You don't need a polished performance, but you do need to connect as a real person who is friendly and approachable. Lauren Clement has a clear message in one of my favourite quotes: 'The brain sees brands with emotion so be clear about how you want to make people feel.'[2] When presenting ideas and opinions, your audience is more likely to trust you if you resonate with them.

It's the person behind the brand that counts. So, what does this mean? Forget about the word brand. Let's replace it with reputation.

> **66** Your brand name is only as good as your reputation."
>
> —*Sir Richard Branson, English business magnate*[3]

A personal brand is about perception and how other people see you. If you are a confident communicator, you will be seen as more professional. People will often make up a story about you, and it might not be one that you like. But everybody has a different point of view and all you can do is be yourself and express yourself well. If we are present and in the moment, our communication is spontaneous, fluent, convincing and calm. This is the ultimate aim when we are communicating.

Trust is the foundation of communication and if it's broken it takes years to rebuild. My job is to help people improve their performance so any audience, whether it be one person or one thousand, sits on the edge of the seat taking in every word because they are inspired by you and trust you. If your body language is spontaneous and natural, your audience will find it easier to trust you. If your voice is strong and animated, people instantly believe that you're passionate about the topic. It's easy for an audience to tell if you are not being yourself.

People trust you when you are sincere, and you will trust yourself more when you are relaxed and free of tension.

Expressive body language

66 It is natural to be nervous, but it's an art not to show it."
—*Laurence Olivier, English actor*[4]

Non-verbal communication is a study within itself. Correct posture and an expressive face make for a lively performance. You are judged within the blink of an eye. Many of my clients start their first session with me feeling and looking nervous. This is normal, given the fact that they are in a room with a stranger who is unpacking the reasons for them being there. It sounds a bit like going into psychoanalysis for the first time, right? Well, it feels like that from where I sit as well, but I listen with no judgment and try not to interrupt. As my client delivers their presentation I am filming and looking at their body language. That's when I know how frightened or confident this person is. Seeing their progress after playing back each performance is something I never get tired of. It's astonishing how much a client will improve within two hours. I watch people unclasp their stiff arms from behind their safe backs and settle. I watch awkward, twisted, terrified feet uncurl and become grounded. I watch shy, inhibited eyes staring at the ceiling connect with mine. I watch frozen, neutral faces smile and move their 30 muscles. I watch a person stretch up from a hunched posture to a straight spine and tall stance. I watch flapping, clammy, anxious fingers relax and uncurl. I watch repetitive jerky arm movements turn into fluid, natural gestures in synergy with spoken words. In these moments I am a silent witness encouraging people to unlearn their habits. Sometimes that's a big ask, but I am proud when I see the changes being made week after week, month after month.

A client of mine, Beth, was quiet, composed and highly intelligent. The content of her presentation was excellent, but her body language told a different story. In her first session with me she absentmindedly moved back and forth like a rocking chair. When I played back her performance she realized how important it was to have some stillness and only move when there was a reason for moving. When she breathed correctly and remained still and less nervous, her movements became natural. She looked calm, centred and confident. She no longer looked rattled. I cannot teach anyone how to smile; it has to come from the heart. But the more Beth relaxed, the more a smile emerged on her softened face. I received an email from Beth after she gave her presentation at an international conference, where she received positive feedback.

For some of you, gesturing might not feel natural, but we need to be animated to connect with others. As master personal brand strategist, Susan Chritton, states, 'Act as if you are always on display because you are.'[5]

A powerful voice

Why is your voice so important to your personal brand? Putting it simply: people will react to you differently because of the sound of your voice. Many of my clients speak quietly in the first half an hour of a session, not because they are shy, but because this is a learnt habit. There is nothing wrong with a quiet voice but if you want to be perceived as confident and capable you need to turn up the volume and sound like you are comfortable and strong. It's almost as though we carry our personalities in our voices. I recommend going to a local voice class at any community drama or performing arts school for some dedicated study with a professional voice tutor. This will not only build your confidence but will build your personal brand. The way you speak and the way you sound will influence the way people respond to you. What I sometimes see in my classes are strained or hesitant voices, so I devote time to teach simple and easy relaxation exercises that clients can practise or use at home.

When presenting yourself and your personal brand authentically, your voice is often the thing that can give you away. Whether you are putting on a brave face and speaking too loudly or whispering because you are afraid, the people around you will notice. It's really important to speak confidently and clearly. Practising and finding your authentic voice will make a difference and this can be done in a number of ways. Judy Apps is a professional voice coach and author living in Dorking, Surrey, in England. She writes about authenticity in one of her four books, *Voice and Speaking Skills for Dummies*, and refers to 'the voice of the gut'. She suggests making the 'ohm' sound used in meditation. For years I have been producing this simple sound in meditation classes and I strongly recommend you follow this exercise to practise finding your voice of the gut. Judy believes this sound is 'entirely free of self-consciousness, role-playing and any other posturing or ego-positioning'.[6] She recommends listening to the actor Ian McKellen in the epic film series, *Lord of The Rings*, as he has a gut tone. This gut tone will be different for everyone. The key is to practise finding your own voice.

Often, when we are anxious, we breathe more shallowly, from the upper chest and not the diaphragm. This can cause you to run out of air and your voice to sound tense. A large majority of my clients have told me that they don't like their own voice when they hear themselves. Making friends with your voice is important because it's your voice and no one else's. You can't sound relaxed if you are worried about your pitch, tone or accent. By working with a vocal technician, you will start to understand that the voice is like an instrument and you can change the way you sound. Diction and clarity are what matter when presenting. Your audience needs to hear the words, so pronunciation of the vowel sounds is vital. People want to hear a passionate and confident vocal range. If you are expressive and enthusiastic you project more energy and your messages will be conveyed more powerfully.

Listen to powerful and persuasive voices in speeches online (for instance TED Talks) and write down what you consider to be a good voice. What voice engages you? Does this speaker use pauses often? Is there a variety of pitch in the voice — meaning highs and lows and no monotone? Does this speaker have passion in their voice? Is it expressive? Now tape your own voice reading prose, a poem, a speech or a short newspaper article, and play it back. Which adjective would you use to describe your voice? Would it be a voice that is influential, reluctant, excited, boring or positive? You can train your voice by experimenting and changing it to suit your style and your personal brand.

There is an exercise I often use with many clients and I encourage you to try this out now.

Exercise

Grab your smartphone and set up either the video or voice recorder. Now record yourself as you read aloud the following script: 'Thank you for taking the time to listen to me today. If you invest in our project I promise you will have no regrets; in fact, within a month your brand will soar beyond your wildest dreams.'

Read the script with anger, then again with elation, then while expressing shyness, then with boredom and then with absolute arrogance.

When you play back the recording you will hear the many attitudes that have a different meaning behind the sound.

This acting exercise, which I video and play back to clients, is designed so that a client can hear how they sound and see how body language alters with each different reading. You can control and manage the way you sound when you speak by thinking about the meaning behind the words.

Exercise

Once again, prepare your smartphone to either video or record this exercise. Read the following excerpt from William Shakespeare's *Hamlet* out loud, three times. First, read it as you imagine inspiring an audience. Then repeat it and soothe the audience. Finally, read it with a feeling of warning the audience.

> This above all: to thine own self be true,
> And it must follow, as the night the day,
> Thou canst not then be false to any man.
> Farewell, my blessing season this in thee!"

How did you go? Now listen back to each of the three samples. What do you notice? Actors warm up their voices before each performance, focusing on relaxing and breathing. A relaxed voice will send out a message that you are calm and confident. The reason for warming up the body and voice is to relax you and prepare you to be more focused before you present. The haka has to be the most public warm-up for the All Blacks and gets their minds ready for the job. Let's take a lesson from these rugby athletes and warm up so our spirits are also in good form.

I strongly recommend that you apply these exercises to your next speech or business presentation.

Looking after your mind

> " Our mind spins out an endless fantasy. We live in a dream dominated by the stories we tell ourselves: stories about who we are, about what people think of us, about what we are going to do."
>
> —*James William Coleman, American sociologist and Buddhist scholar*[7]

Your inner critic is a disturbing nuisance, so tell it to go away. Or as they say in Italy, '*Basta!* Enough, stop!' Distorting the truth in our minds becomes habit-forming and we need to listen more to our loved ones and loyal followers who praise us for the good work we do when we present. When people overcome their fear of speaking in public they regain their authority and confidence, which in turn makes for a stronger presenter. Stage fright is not a disease and you will not die even if you faint or pass out from nerves. We are not our thoughts and we can retrain our mind to look after our body. Learning how to present in a powerful way is important, because you need to be able to articulate, clearly and authoritatively, what it is that you do.

Gerard, one of my clients, is a master mariner and he recounted the story of how he once stood on his ship, briefing the crew, when his throat constricted and he felt suddenly unwell. When he attempted to speak, words literally wouldn't come out of his mouth, so he asked for a glass of water. Gerard had given thousands of speeches in his career and was used to a leadership role and giving commands, although at the time of this episode he was under massive amounts of work stress. He had no idea what was happening to him and didn't for a moment consider he was experiencing an anxiety attack. When I talked with Gerard in our first phone call, I discussed the fight or flight response when in situations of acute stress. In the primordial response of fight or flight, we are getting ready to defend our territory, like an animal who is about to be preyed upon. We feel afraid. Do we stay or run?

> 66 The instinctive physiological response to a threatening situation, which readies one either to resist forcibly or to run away. Humans, like all animals, have an inborn stress alarm system that initiates a fight or flight response to stressful situations."
>
> —*fight or flight definition*, Oxford English Dictionary[8]

The first time an anxiety attack occurs can be terrifying. But trust me, if this happens to you, you are not going crazy and are not in danger. This is something that millions of people experience daily. Take deep breaths and if you are giving a presentation, return to a simple mantra in your mind, 'I am calm'. Repeat this over and over in your mind. No one is going to hurt you, you are safe and your audience will appreciate you taking the time to speak to them — even if what you're doing is as simple as briefing your crew on a ship.

Self-esteem and self-belief

❝ When you're different, sometimes you don't see
the millions of people who accept you for what you
are. All you notice is the person who doesn't."

—*Jodi Picoult, American author*[9]

Facing your fear and staring at it in the mirror is confronting but you can step up, make sacrifices and become a riveting communicator. High-performing athletes show up as dedicated and disciplined performers in all areas of their lives. I have high expectations of my clients to do the same and transform themselves into 'high-performance presenters' through consistent practice. Experiencing a sense of high self-esteem is the greatest feeling anyone can have and a great weapon in your arsenal, because you are not relying on others' opinions to feel alright.

We are knocked off our perch so easily when things go wrong in our lives. Self-doubt creeps in and thoughts spiral out of control in our busy and often tortured minds. When we are criticized, we dwell on the negatives for far too long and forget about all the times we nailed a presentation and got rave reviews. Conversely, what about a meeting you have attended, where you shared your point of view in a complicated way and were met with blank faces and no one knew what you were talking about? What about that time you forgot your colleague's name and you stood embarrassed as you were about to make an introduction at an important event? What about when you forgot to name the sponsor on the stage when you were the MC at a conference? We need to forgive ourselves, as we are only human and mistakes happen. That's how we learn.

My belief is that when we know who we are and feel comfortable in our skin we are not performing for someone else. We are just being. I think one of the best ways to become confident is to attend drama classes and take every speaking opportunity available. Also, being filmed so you can play it back and critique yourself is a great help and essential for improvement. Aaron, my auctioneer client, has every presentation filmed by a student so he can play it back, self-critique and improve. He raises the bar every time.

Another option is to find a reliable and talented coach to work with you on your presentation skills, to increase self-belief while motivating you to develop. Any dazzling moment when you exude confidence will make you look and sound more credible and you will increase your chances of expanding your business network by opening up new doors. There's always more to learn, especially if you are a business leader or have a public profile. So don't leave this too long on your to-do list. Start now and get into action.

I hold in the highest esteem people who ask for help, not only for their courage in putting themselves under the microscope but because they are declaring an intention to grow and, in so doing, increase their self-worth. In my work as a performance coach it's my job to make people feel safe, comfortable and unafraid to take risks. Often, potential clients find me through my website, so that first impression of professionalism mixed with kindness is critical in giving people confidence about meeting me face to face. The new client might arrive with hesitance but at least feeling like they already know me a little from my online profile. Shyness, fragility, anxiety, inhibition and nervousness walk in my door and I never take this for granted. Trusting a stranger after only a digital 'meet and greet' comes with risk and more often than not there is trepidation. I always acknowledge new clients for their courage and faith when they hire me as their trainer without meeting me first, and then give themselves fully to the process.

Being memorable

66 The holy grail of a presentation is to transport an audience to another place."

—*Carmine Gallo, American author and columnist*[10]

Being a persuasive speaker exponentially increases your chances of having a stronger personal brand, especially in the digital world, because you can reach more people, which builds your profile. People will notice you, talk about you and remember your name when they are no longer with you and they are likely to go home or back to the office and run a digital search to know more about you. So your goal is to be remembered for that vibrant speech you made, which will inspire further digital investigation of you and your brand.

None of us are perfect orators and everyone who speaks will have delivered a speech that fell flat, prompting a sudden overwhelming longing to crawl under the carpet and disappear. There is an expectation for business leaders to be good at presenting and many of my clients admit having deliberately orchestrated matters to get out of delivering those big speeches, passing the task to someone in their team who is more natural in the art of speaking. The problem with this strategy is that you are passing on a chance to shine and an opportunity for people to know and remember you. Try not to let some unrealistic idea of perfection (or imperfection, as the case might be) get in the way of your appointment in the limelight. Remember, you need a little of that light to showcase your own personal story and brand, so try not to squander the opportunity by giving in to fear.

As part of my program 'Creating Presence', we perform an exercise using props where the participants tell a story. Each person chooses three props, from a bag of hundreds, to create a story about their role in the workplace. They are given one to two minutes to come up with a short presentation about what it is that they bring to their jobs.

Somebody might hold up a big red velvet heart, another person might hold up a small plastic hammer, another person might hold up a plastic champagne bottle or a bright yellow worker's hard hat; all hold different meanings for different people. The point of the exercise is to hone your storytelling skills, to paint pictures by improvising in a short timeframe with little preparation. Often, using props can free you up and stimulate your imagination to be a bit more creative and spontaneous.

Here is an example of part of one of the most memorable uses of props from a workshop participant. Harriet's stories were so memorable that I insisted she transcribe her two-minute presentation and use it as part of her 'elevator pitch'.

Harriet's example: (Harriet picks up a feather duster and starts speaking) 'What is this? If you ask a three-year-old they could probably come up with 50 ideas for what this might represent. If you ask an 80-year-old, they might be able to come up with twenty uses. If you ask an eighteen-year-old they could probably come up with two. This means that we are dumbing down creativity in our children by having them in an education system that speaks to conformity and being told what to do, as opposed to thinking outside the box and coming up with different ways of doing things. So my mission is to provide learning environments that allow children to explore and follow their natural urge of being curious, which links to finding out what they are passionate about and, therefore, finding their true calling.'

During the two-day course, Harriet presented as one of the more hesitant participants and was rather quiet. So she surprised us all in this exercise because she was so expressive, heartfelt, real and personal. Even though she wasn't the most confident speaker in the course, her content and meanings behind the props made her memorable in the exercise.

Short videos

Most of us have a short attention span compounded by the 21st century reality of being very busy and time poor. You'll be well served to know how to tell your story in fewer than 100 words. In short bursts, we can be transported into the world of a client, future business partner or employer and build a relationship faster. As an expert in your field, it's important to be accessible. You want people to feel comfortable picking up the phone and calling you.

My advice is to have a short, well-rehearsed video on your website to showcase the real you. It's also a good idea to include captions on your video to reinforce your key messages. If you are shy or introverted, get some training and ask for professional feedback. If you have a friend or contact who has a background in journalism or copywriting it's worth asking them to help write your script. From my experience, the best scriptwriters are journalists. They know how to chip, chop, trash and edit those long-winded sentences. Professor Emeritus at the University of Missouri School of Journalism, Dr Don Ranly, puts it in plain terms: 'Make it brief, make it useful and make it sharable'.[11]

Credentials

If a prospective client asks you to send some examples of you performing publicly — for example, making a speech or sitting on a panel — it's a good idea to be organized to direct them to your website or another digital platform to sample your work. I have some great videos on my website and people find them useful when researching me. Be advised, however, to refresh these often as you don't want old and dated work being showcased if it no longer properly represents you and your brand. Sometimes, though, old interviews may be useful because the content has original meaning, or maybe it shows a breakthrough moment. You will be your own best judge on which material best serves your brand's message.

Another tip: if you have been interviewed for radio or TV, post the interviews on your business Facebook page and link them to your website. Get a copy of the original file from the producer so you can file it and use it again and again. Stick to a plan and list all the ways you can share your public interviews. We live in a dynamic digital playground, so you need to be visible.

Energy: it's show time!

Food, sleep and exercise are three vital ingredients for an energetic performance. Actors often refer to the phrase 'it's show time', which means, 'we are on!' You have to bring energy to any presentation, either online or offline. I'm admittedly bossy with my clients the week before an important presentation, making sure their preparation and lead-up facilitates the best performance they have in them.

Consider rehearsing, perhaps filming yourself on a smartphone or tablet and looking back at it. Maybe you could enrol a friend to run a second pair of eyes over your performance and give you honest feedback. Remember my earlier analogy of a high-performance athlete? It's practice that counts and the more you do, the more likely you will win in your personal game.

Role models: radiating confidence

66 We convince by our presence."

—*Walt Whitman, American poet*[12]

Interesting role models who have a presence when they speak are worth their weight in gold. Watch them interact with an audience and listen to their confident voices. What captures you?

In my twenties, learning about presence as an actor was both liberating and excruciating. My mind was living in the past and future so much of the time. What helped me to be more present was meditation, which actors often use to free the mind of stress. Business leaders can learn from actors. Having presence comes from the inside — you can't fake it; you have to find it.

If you want to be seen as an expert in your field, then you must invest time in expressing your personal brand whether online or offline. Learning from more experienced speakers is an excellent way to lift your act and improve your communication style. By sharing something personal about yourself in a sincere way you will connect with your audience. Relaxed body language, direct eye contact, warm smiles and expressive gestures hold our attention. Relevant, well thought out anecdotes that paint pictures make for more memorable content. A vibrant, confident speaker doesn't rely on notes or PowerPoint and is unafraid to share something of who they are.

Notice the times when you are more engaged with speakers. We buy from the heart and are moved when people show their feelings and connect with emotions. It's not about impressing an audience; it's about connecting with them.

Star speaker: a case study

When it comes to developing a personal brand, it doesn't get much bigger than Oprah Winfrey. When she speaks, the world listens, engages and connects across all media platforms. Best known for *The Oprah Winfrey Show* (the highest rated television show of its kind in history), the American media proprietor, talk-show host, actress, producer, author and philanthropist is quite simply a 'global media queen'. Oprah is frequently described as the world's most powerful woman.

I love Oprah Winfrey and really relate to her story, her style and her politics. I love that she is grounded and insightful and I revere the way she listens to, learns from and shares her wisdom with others. Above all else, I respect the success she has created for herself and for others. Oprah says, 'All my life I have wanted to lead people to an empathy space, to a gratitude space; I want us all to fulfil our greatest potential. To find our calling, and summon the courage to live it.'[13]

On 7 January 2018 Oprah delivered a speech at the Golden Globe Awards. This was a wonderful piece of oratory that will rank as one of the most remarkable and memorable speeches of a generation. Oprah is an extremely seasoned performer, so there's a lot to learn from studying her. I encourage you to take a look at the speech on YouTube and then read my comments below.

First up, she grabbed the opportunity to say something significant about sexual harassment in the entertainment industry, and the #MeToo campaign. She took it with both hands and owned it! Oprah has lived this stuff and campaigned against it all her life, so she was able to write and deliver a completely authentic speech. She didn't need to create an aura of credibility; she was able to talk from her heart and her own lived experience. Even better, she positioned a speech that was perfect for the occasion, providing personal anecdotes, historical context and hope for the future.

The speech opened with Oprah as a little girl sitting on the linoleum floor of her mother's house in Milwaukee, watching Anne Bancroft present the Oscar for Best Actor to Sidney Poitier at the 36th Academy Awards. 'Up to the stage came the most elegant man I had ever seen.

I remember his tie was white and of course his skin was black — I'd never seen a black man being celebrated like that.'

Great technique: she takes us into her world and helps us see another point of view.

Oprah continued. 'I have tried many, many times to explain what a moment like that means to a little girl, a kid watching from the cheap seats as my mom came through the door bone tired from cleaning other people's houses.' This is great use of language.

She noted the significance of time and history and showed her ability to think about the audience she wanted to reach: 'In 1982 Sidney received the Cecil B. DeMille award right here at the Golden Globes and it is not lost on me that at this moment, there are some little girls watching as I become the first black woman to be given this same award.'

Acknowledgments can be a very powerful part of your speech. In her speech Oprah's were expertly framed, inclusive and genuine. This is a chance for you to bond with the audience.

From here she returned to one of her key life messages and a key part of her 'brand': 'What I know for sure is that speaking your truth is the most powerful tool we all have. I'm especially proud and inspired by all the women who have felt strong enough and empowered enough to speak up and share their personal stories.' She reminded us that the #MeToo story stretches far beyond the entertainment industry: 'It's one that transcends any culture, geography, race, religion, politics or workplace.' She then continued to build momentum. 'I want tonight to express gratitude to all the women who have endured years of abuse and assault because they, like my mother, had children to feed, bills to pay and dreams to pursue. They're the women whose names we'll never know ... They are domestic workers and farm workers, they are working in factories and they work in restaurants, in academia, medicine and science. They are part of the world of tech and politics and business. They're our athletes in the Olympics and they're our soldiers in the military.'

Then with perfect timing she changes pace, bringing in a powerful story about Recy Taylor, a young wife and mother, who back in 1944 was abducted, blindfolded and raped by six white men. Oprah recounted how the men threatened to kill her if she told anyone but Recy Taylor had enough guts to report her story to Rosa Parks, then a young worker at the NAACP (National Association for the Advancement of Coloured People). While they both sought justice for her case, they were unsuccessful and the men were never prosecuted. This is a powerful reminder that violence and abuse towards women is not a new story. Oprah made the story more poignant by telling us that Recy Taylor had recently died 'just shy of her 98th birthday'. Building to the climax of the speech she then brings in her now famous refrain: 'For too long women have not been heard or believed if they dared to speak their truth to the power of those men. But their time is up. Their time is up. Their time is up.' The repetition was compelling and in delivering the last 'their time is up', her voice raised in celebration and with conviction.

Great storytellers always bring their stories to a conclusion, using the conclusion to drive home their key messages. 'I just hope that Recy Taylor died knowing that her truth, like the truth of so many other women who were tormented in those years and even now are tormented, goes marching on. It was somewhere in Rosa Parks' heart almost eleven years later, when she made the decision to stay seated on the bus in Montgomery and it is here with every woman who chooses to say, "MeToo". And with every man — every man who chooses to listen.'

Finally, Oprah 'ties it up with a bow', leaving a strong, hopeful message. 'So I want all the girls watching here and now to know that a new day is on the horizon. And when that new day finally dawns, it will be because of a lot of magnificent women, many of whom are right here in this room tonight, and some pretty phenomenal men, fighting hard to make sure they become the leaders who take us to the time when nobody has to say "MeToo" again. Thank you.'

Winfrey's was a speech that will go down in the history books of 21st century oratory. Just a couple of days after its delivery, its YouTube clip had over 1 million views. And within hours of Oprah taking to the Golden Globes stage, political pundits and the Twitter world erupted in speculation as to whether she was gearing up for a presidential run in 2020. The speech got rave reviews pretty much across the board. One critic called it 'unifying, powerful, inclusive, forward-looking, rousing, empowering, inspiring and embodied in the best tradition of American oratory'.[14]

So what has this speech got to do with your personal brand and why am I including it in this chapter? Oprah's presentation has all the hallmarks of a dynamic speech. She has a presence when she speaks because she's had years of experience and has perfected the art of powerful public speaking. She has made it part of her brand to tell the stories of others. She found her niche at a young age and created a career representing the downtrodden, the disempowered and the underdogs of life. She is truly masterful in embodying her personal brand and communicating it like almost no one else on the planet.

66 If I'm remembered for having done a few good things, and if my presence here has sparked some good energies, that's plenty."

—*Sidney Poitier, American actor*[15]

7

Networking your personal brand

66 The guiding principle of networking is to
give first and receive second."

—*Elizabeth Asquith Bibesco, British author and poet*[1]

Why is it necessary to network when building our personal brand?
First, let's attempt to demystify the word networking. *The Oxford English
Dictionary* defines this sometimes dreaded or irritating word as, 'A group
of people who exchange information and contacts for professional or
social purposes'.[2] This sentence is not exactly motivating or enticing.
For me, networking is when a group of people in a room meet each

other for the first time for a reason. So why do we get so uptight about this terminology? After all, we have been socializing for centuries.

Some of my clients with chronic aversion to the idea of formal 'networking' playfully ask me if it wouldn't be easier to sit up in bed on a Sunday morning in their pyjamas drinking hot coffee, munching croissants and signing up more LinkedIn business pals. This way they wouldn't have to leave the comfort of their cosy duvet and goose pillow and yet they could still build contacts and show off an impressive network list. Do I recommend this? Definitely not. Networking requires effort and we all need to do it no matter what our job is or our background. For some of you, the thought of going into a room with strangers fills your body and mind with dread and fear. You are not alone. In fact, I'll wager that half the people in the room feel exactly the same way as you. It's my intention in writing this chapter to help you feel more at ease when you are networking, and to share my knowledge and tips to help you conquer any fears. These pages are aimed at helping you become a natural networker in order to help you grow your personal brand.

Many of my clients know I'm passionate about connecting people and a week doesn't go by without me introducing a friend to a client. My enthusiasm comes from many years of building a professional network based on repeat business and referrals, and from attending endless networking events even when I have been reluctant to go. It's essential to foster this skill if you are serious about having a strong personal brand. Networking is something everyone can learn — most of us are not born natural networkers. Social media networking works to a certain extent but do not underestimate the importance of building and growing relationships from meeting people face to face. If you rely on the digital world to increase your network, you will miss out on cultivating deeper business relationships. My belief is that you need both to grow your brand and business.

The reason for going to a certain function might be to get a new job, speak to stakeholders or increase productivity in your current company. Every single time you meet a stranger and engage in a meaningful conversation you are on the road to creating a new relationship that could transform your business and possibly even the rest of your life. This may sound dramatic but, based on my experience, anything is possible when you show up to an event. Never underestimate the power of being at a conference or function with hundreds of potential customers who might need you and you them. Networking simply increases your chances of turning dreams and goals into reality.

At home, we feel comfortable when we host our guests because we're in our comfort zone — we feel safe and relaxed, and the situation is not artificial. We are in charge and there's already a foundation of trust and a sense of belonging. But when we go out into the world to network we don't have our security blanket with us and often we are alone, without family or friends to prop us up. But everything in life has an objective or a goal and the same goes with networking. Why are you going to this function? Have you been told by your boss to go out and generate more new business? Do you want to be the top biller in the company? Have you been told to stop lounging on the couch watching Netflix and go and chase that investor money for your start-up business? Whatever the reason, do not buy in to any of your excuses. They are all tales that you tell yourself. I recommend making a list of reasons why you are attending an event. What's in it for you and what's in it for the people you meet? You have a great deal to give, so get to work.

Networking did not come naturally to me when I first set up a business. I had to work very hard to focus on making an effort to turn up and turn it on. I worked out ways of making myself feel at ease. For example, the first thing I used to do to calm myself down was to chat to the hospitality staff while I got a glass of wine before going to shake hands with a complete stranger. But in order to feel as comfortable as possible I learnt very quickly that my first step should be to plan ahead. There's no point in turning up without an intention. It's that probing, basic question again: 'Why am I here?'

Planning

66 Planning is bringing the future into the present
so that you can do something about it now."
—*Alan Lakein, American author*[3]

If you plan ahead, you will have a reason for going to the event and that will motivate you to make an effort. You are going there to achieve something. You are going there to have stimulating conversations and expand your horizons. Just think of it as extending your group of friends. In other words, it's not scary because you can usually find things in common with people.

The first step in planning ahead is to access a guest list before you turn up. If you want to come away with new business, look at the list of companies before the event and write down the names of two people you want to meet and endeavour to find and talk to them.

It's also important to find out the dress code so you don't under- or over-dress for an event. Make sure you don't walk out of your office or home without your business cards — it's better to have too many than not enough. Also, carry a pen in your pocket or purse. Always be on time. It's easier to meet people at the beginning of the event than walk into a sea of suits with everyone already engaging in buzzy chatter, where you will have to pluck up the courage to interrupt.

If you are attending a conference, read the brochure or the information that has been emailed to you and plan well ahead, studying the guest speakers. Remember you will have opportunities to meet people in smaller groups if there are breakout meetings or discussion groups. Afternoon and morning tea breaks are often a leisurely time to introduce yourself to people in a less formal setting. The mistake people sometimes make is going straight to their phones to check messages in the breaks instead of fraternizing with others at the event. During a break, I usually ask a stranger something like, 'What do you think of the speaker?' We are expected to be spontaneous but it's often easier if we have some stock planned questions to ease the strain.

How to start

> 66 Take the initiative. Be proactive. If you want to rock your relationship results, it is going to take action, effort, initiative and choosing to get in the game — so, step up, step out and show up!"
>
> —*Susan C. Young, American author[4]*

If you are painstakingly shy or an introvert, it's best to arrive to an event ten minutes before anyone else. This ensures that the next person who arrives is going to head straight for you and they will have to do all the work (which might help to put you at ease). If you enter the room after others, get your glass of water or wine (not too much) and make a pact with yourself that you are going to walk up to the first friendly face, smile, shake their hand and introduce yourself. If you find yourself feeling anxious or nervous, take a deep breath and have a pep talk with yourself (not out loud): 'This is easy, come on, I can do this!' I appreciate that if you suffer from social anxiety this is not an easy process. It's a work in progress and it will take time. You've got your names of the two people you want to meet, so go out and search for them. You know what they look like because you've done your research. You know what they do because you've studied their LinkedIn pages. You could even stand close to the table where people pick up their name tags and ask the host to introduce you.

Make a decision to leave all your doubts and negative thoughts outside the door. You must walk in with a positive attitude thinking that it will be an enjoyable event. You should expect it to be easy and to come away with some good contacts. I used to tell myself at every networking function I attended that I was going to come away with new business and I always did because I went in with a positive mind-set. I treated it like a fun game that I wanted to win.

Ice-breaker conversations

66 Listen with curiosity. Speak with honesty. Act with integrity. The greatest problem with communication is we don't listen to understand. We listen to reply. When we listen with curiosity, we don't listen with the intent to reply. We listen for what's behind the words."

—*Roy T. Bennett, author*[5]

The biggest mistake at any networking event is to talk too much and talk about yourself. Talking at people doesn't encourage the other person to warm to you. Make it easy on yourself and ask a question, or even two or three. Be curious. This generosity of spirit will mean the other person feels listened to and feels valued. If there is one thing I've learnt about human beings, it's that everybody wants and needs to be heard. When I talk to new clients they tell me that they don't feel comfortable making small talk and they say they feel inauthentic and insincere when they do chit chat at functions. My answer to that is to get interested in what the other person is saying and listen from a place of understanding and compassion. You can discover a meeting point and find things in common. Don't be egocentric. Egocentric people have no regard for others and people often find themselves making a sudden exit to the bathroom (or finding another excuse) when in the presence of someone who shows no interest in them. Check in with yourself and ask, 'Am I talking too much about myself? Am I really listening? Am I present?' Think of networking as an opportunity to give rather than focusing on what you are getting out of it.

Sometimes people only think of networking as a way to sell a product, find a new job or gain more new business. This is a mistake. Make connections with people and create meaningful relationships by listening to their stories. There are many ways to build rapport. You can solve problems, share your contacts, give suggestions and ideas or invite someone to an event you are going to the following month. I am a very positive and proactive person who thinks always in terms of human relations. When I meet people for the first time, I usually think, 'What can I do to make this person's work and life better? What do I have that could be useful and helpful to him or her?' The more you give, the more you'll receive. If you go out of your way to help someone, without expecting anything in return, at some stage of your life this person will possibly return the favour.

Asking questions

66 Only networking when you have to, means you're more likely to feel anxious and stress yourself out. Rather than focusing on what you need to get out of the event, try to think of what you can offer others from the experience."

—*Ben Dattner, Professor of Psychology, New York University*[6]

I encourage using open-ended questions when talking with strangers at an event. These help to generate conversations rather than a simple yes or no answer. Here are some examples.

1. 'What are you enjoying most about this event?'

2. 'Tell me about your work; what do you do?'

3. 'What's the highlight of your job?'

4. 'What's the biggest challenge you face in your role at work?'

5. After checking their nametag: 'I see you work for an accountancy firm; what is your role there?'

6. Think about what is currently going on in the world and start there. Be up-to-date with the latest news so you've got plenty of general knowledge. Sports offers a range of safe questions, for example, 'Did you see the game last Saturday?'

Questions to avoid

1. 'How old are you?'

2. 'Can you do me a favour and find my friend a job?' This person does not know you, let alone your mate!

3. 'So who did you vote for in the election last week?' Don't ever ask a stranger who they vote for. It's okay to talk about politics but you can slide down a slippery slope very fast if you are engaging with someone whose political opinions are opposite to yours.

4. 'How much money do you make in a year?'

5. 'How can you help me?' Don't ask this or any other version of this.

> 66 Remember, networking isn't about selling; in fact, it's not about talking. Networking is about listening. The best networkers are the ones who are able to build relationships and invest time finding out about others."
>
> —*Catriona Pollard, founder, CP Communications Australia*[7]

Inevitably you're going to come across people who are hard to talk to. But don't give up. You have no idea what stress this person might be under in their life. And sometimes people just aren't talkative. Keep on asking questions and don't be afraid of the silences. Sometimes we fill up the space with lots of noise and chitter-chatter because we feel ill at ease. If you are really struggling, this is where your elevator pitch comes in to play.

Elevator pitch

> 66 If you can't explain it simply, you don't
> understand it well enough."
> —*Albert Einstein*[8]

An elevator pitch is a short, succinct, carefully written and well-rehearsed description of what you do. The name 'elevator pitch' reflects the idea that it should be possible to deliver the pitch in the time it takes an elevator to reach its destination (approximately 30 to 60 seconds). Your mother, your grandmother or a twelve-year-old should be able to understand what you're saying in your elevator pitch, so use everyday language and avoid technical jargon. The idea at the start is to really hook the listener by creating an innovative definition of what you do. It's worth practising because the idea behind this quick pitch is that the person listening will be left wanting to know more.

Creating an elevator pitch for themselves is the one exercise that my clients often struggle with, so do not despair if you are challenged. Practise with someone who does not understand your business, then you will have to work harder at your pitch. Ask for feedback. Earlier on in my career, I used to say that I was a presentation coach. Now, when people ask me what I do, my opening words are, 'I help people shine on the stage.' And that's only two seconds' worth of breath. It surprises me that this follows with a list of curious questions like, 'What kind of a stage?' and 'Do you mean a business stage?'

Ronald Reagan, former US President and a former actor, was known for his succinct questioning during his summary in the debate with Jimmy Carter during the 1980 presidential campaign. He asked the audience, 'Ask yourself, are you better off now than you were four years ago?'[9] This was a great strategy. Try starting your elevator pitch with a question and see what response you get. Another well-known elevator pitch opening question comes from Apple's founder Steve Jobs, when he was trying to persuade John Sculley to leave PepsiCo for Apple Inc. 'Do you want to spend the rest of your life selling sugared water, or do you want a chance to change the world?'[10]

You can spend a full day on an elevator pitch until you are satisfied that it captures the essence of you. It's a good use of your time and professional budget to sign up for a course to get your creative juices flowing and unlock a new narrative. I encourage my clients to change their pitch every few years, and certainly when you start a new job you should refresh and rethink your elevator pitch.

Ten tips for your elevator pitch

1. Have a hook in the first ten to fifteen seconds.

2. Pitch yourself, not your ideas.

3. Avoid business jargon — don't use technical terminology.

4. Highlight what you have done — concrete accomplishments or skills.

5. Memorize your elevator pitch so it rolls off your tongue.

6. Use short sentences.

7. Practise it by writing it down.

8. Rehearse and deliver it in front of the mirror or to a friend or colleague.

9. Smile and don't be aggressive.

10. Remember to listen to feedback when your pitch is over.

Breaking into a group

There are a few things people are generally afraid of when trying to break into a group. Some people are worried about not being able to contribute to the conversation. The key here is to listen. Don't feel as if you have to talk, but if you are struggling to find something to say, ask a question. Some people don't want to be rude and interrupt. If I break into a group I will say, 'I'm sorry to interrupt your conversation, please carry on.' This always works for me. It's about basic manners. Trust your intuition.

During the writing of this book I went to an exclusive function at the invitation of a new client I had met the day before. Out of 200 people at that function, I had only previously met two. During the event, I was standing outside a small circle of people, waiting for them to notice me and motion to me to join them. They were standing so close together, engaging in chatter, so it didn't feel appropriate to break in by tapping someone on the shoulder. I felt extremely uncomfortable because they didn't let me in. I bravely went over to a different group and introduced myself. I held out my hand to shake the hands of everyone in the huddle and it went smoothly from there. It reminded me of how awkward people can feel when they don't know anybody. Even seasoned networkers like me can feel momentarily uncomfortable.

Things to remember

- I recommend that people who don't enjoy networking go to events with another person — but don't use them as a crutch. When you start to feel more confident, start going alone so you have no choice but to talk to others.

- Remember that the person (or people) you are talking to often feels as uncomfortable as you. The more you practise networking the better you become at breaking into a group and working a room.

- The first thing to do when breaking into a group is to make sure you are standing opposite someone so they can actually see you and make eye contact. Or gently stand very close to someone without invading their personal space.

- If I've spotted someone I know, I gently tap their elbow and whisper a 'hello' and they let me in. At that stage, my colleague or friend will usually introduce me to the group and if they don't, I will introduce myself.

- Check your business cards before the event to make sure they are clean, and use a business card case so they do not crease or get marked. A dirty business card doesn't do your reputation any good.

- When I am talking with people in a group, I use my peripheral vision and when I see someone outside of the group, I will let them in and host that person. But not everyone does this. Think of yourself as the perfect friendly host at all times when you are in a group, and look out for those on their own. Your kindness will be noted by the person you have hosted, and probably others in the group, too.

Tips for making a good impression

66 I've learned that people will forget what you said, I've learnt that people will forget what you did, but people will never forget how you made them feel."

—*Maya Angelou, American activist, poet and author*[11]

Eye contact

Making eye contact with the person you're talking to shows that you are interested and helps you to focus on the person when you are listening to them. An annoying habit is when the person talking to you is looking over your shoulder at somebody else in the room. This is disrespectful and doesn't facilitate a trusting start. If you are looking over the person's shoulder at somebody else, you are not making a good impression. It tells the person you're speaking to that they don't matter, that there's someone more interesting in the room or that you don't really want to be talking to them.

Some studies say that you are more memorable if you maintain good eye contact with someone you do not know well. My experience has taught me the other person is more focused and present if I make eye contact. Practise and become self-aware, and notice when you divert your eyes away from the person you are talking to. Often it's simply habit, especially when we are feeling uncomfortable. It's easy when we are in love but not so easy with strangers. But do try to stay present.

The handshake

The handshake is your first point of physical contact, and is a polite gesture that says, 'It's great to meet you'. Make sure your grip is neither too weak nor too firm. The bone cruncher handshake, for example, is a killer. When I shook hands with a student at a university event after giving a speech once, I physically let out a painful sound because his handshake was so firm it crushed my fingers. I took him aside in a careful and professional way and gave him some feedback. He had no idea of the impact of his firm handshake. I demonstrated how he should shake hands (which is firm but not a bone cruncher) and he was very grateful.

Conversely, an overly weak handshake tells the other person that you lack confidence. I run a workshop called 'The art of the handshake' and I talk about what handshakes mean in different cultures. This is very important both in multicultural countries as well for those doing business with people from countries and cultures different to their own. Indeed, in my own country, New Zealand, sometimes touching nose to nose is a form of a handshake. Do your research and find out what is culturally acceptable and unacceptable. But be careful and don't make assumptions.

Standing too close to the person you're speaking with is also off-putting. It's best to stand an arm's length away from someone so as not to intrude on their personal space.

Smile

A smile is a simple facial movement that requires little effort and puts people at ease. Smile when you first meet someone and they will warm to you and smile back (hopefully). A smile speaks louder than words and says that you are genuinely pleased to meet that person. Some people have what is crudely called a 'resting bitch face'. This person is probably feeling very happy and content but because they are not smiling we can misinterpret their emotions. I've worked with two colleagues who very rarely smiled. Both were professional women who shared the nickname of 'the Ice Queen'. Ironically, they are two of the kindest people I know. So don't make assumptions and don't think the person doesn't like you. But make sure you smile yourself so that people feel comfortable in approaching and speaking with you. Review any videos of yourself speaking at work functions or family events and you will be able to see for yourself if you are coming across as open, friendly, detached, cold or distant. If you smile you immediately put people at ease and your personal brand will be one of warmth and compassion.

Body language

You can send out the wrong signal if you have distracting body language. This could include crossed arms, crossed legs, fidgeting with your watch or rings or looking around the room and not paying attention. Become aware of your body language and make sure it reflects the message you intend. Try to relax and show this by having your arms uncrossed, face the person you're speaking with, look them in the eye and smile. Be careful not to pick food out of your teeth in front of people as it's not a good look and can be off-putting.

Your energy

Turn up to an event with energy. Leave your tired, grumpy self at home — it's not useful and people will not want to meet you if you have a dark, gloomy cloud over you. We are drawn to energetic people and are more likely to want to stay around them. An energetic voice has more passion and enthusiasm. Get extra sleep, drink lots of water and ensure you exercise in the week leading up to a conference or any networking event.

Be curious

When you go to your next networking function have a positive attitude and expect to meet people that you will have things in common with. Take your curious spirit into the room and set a goal to ask as many open-ended questions as you can in order to leave inspired and looking forward to meeting those people again. You'll also come away learning a lot about the people you've talked to, which can help build your relationship.

You're not at a business networking function to negotiate a deal or sign a contract; you are there to get to know other people. At a networking function think personal, not professional. You can sign the contract later!

Making an exit

Remind yourself that you are there to meet more than one person, so be careful not to spend all your time talking with a single person at the event. It might be useful to have some personal goals, for instance, pledging to have three conversations with three new people in an hour. For me, going to any networking event is about business development. The more people I meet, the more relationships I have and the more I grow my business.

When you start to make your exit from a group, find a pause in the conversation and say, 'it was great to meet you all.' Another way to exit a group is to say, 'Would anyone like another drink?' You can come back with the waiter, hand out some drinks and say goodbye. If there are only a few people, hand out some business cards but don't take up too much time. People expect you to leave — after all, it is a networking event so don't feel like you are being rude. Leave with a genuine smile.

Manners

Everyday etiquette applies at a networking event. Be careful not to interrupt somebody's flow in a conversation or talk over them. Concentrate and listen to what people are saying so you can respond properly. Be empathetic.

Manners: basic tips

- Be personable and warm.
- Be interested and sincere.
- Have courage — step out of your comfort zone.
- Ask genuine questions.
- Listen, listen, listen.
- Receive compliments with a kind heart.
- Pay attention to how much alcohol you consume — less is better and makes for sober and intelligent communication.
- Thank people in writing if they send you new business or refer a contact.

Miracles happen

It's almost as though we are conditioned to think of networking events as a chore and a burden rather than an opportunity to meet fascinating people. If we change our attitude, miracles can happen. Many years ago, I ran a not-for-profit organization in the performing arts. At a networking event, I sat next to a man I didn't know, who turned out to be one of the wealthiest men in the country. He was a shy businessman but I quickly built a rapport with him. We talked about our lives and why we were at that event. After the three-day program, we met up for a coffee and he ended up investing money in my organization for the entire duration that I was director. He became a dear friend, a dedicated mentor and my miracle man.

You never know who you will meet, so the important thing is to be in the room and be open.

Follow up

66 Building a professional relationship is a lot
like [building] a romantic one ..."
—*Emdad Khan, graduate consultant at 3 Minute Mile*[12]

Keep your promises and people will remember you as someone who is dependable. Do you ever say to someone, 'I will call you next week' or 'I will email you' and a year later when you bump into this prospective client at another function you are very embarrassed because you did not keep your word? Forgive yourself but apologize and never make empty promises that you cannot keep. Being known as someone who is reliable and has integrity means everything to your reputation. Always follow up the day after a networking function so people remember the conversation they had with you. It might be useful to make a list now of any broken promises and pick up the phone and make amends and recommit. It's never too late to apologise.

Tips when taking contact details

- Always ask for a business card. Often, people feel uncomfortable about asking the stranger permission to call the following week and set up a business meeting. But this is the whole reason that you are there. Simply ask, 'Can I call you to set up a coffee?'

- If they don't have a business card, put their phone number in your phone and send them a text straightaway so they have your number. If you've left your cards at home this is the fastest way of ensuring you have each other's contact details.

- Once you have the prospective client's business card at home, write down certain details on the back of the card straightaway. For example, I write the date and name of the event where I met them, what they look like and where they work. If I promised them that I'd send a business contact, I write it down on the back of the card and send the email straightaway. I also write down the day I said I would call them and I always make that call. Make an action list. If you've promised to do certain things, make a note of them.

- When you arrive home after the event take the time to go through the business cards and look up their company details, so you learn more about them and how you can help each other.

- Business cards can be easy to lose, so be sure to put all contact details in your phone.

Thanks

66 Say thank you, say it often, and say it with meaning."
—*Marne Levine, COO of Instagram*[13]

It is always polite to send a thank you note or email to the host of an event, especially if you haven't paid to attend. After my first book launch I received thank you emails from almost my entire guest list and it meant the world to me. They were mostly clients of mine, as it was a business event, and to this day I regularly work with these people.

Thank people who refer new business or introduce you to a good business contact. New business leads come from someone who respects you and your brand. You might want to send a thank you card by post or even an e-card instead of an email, as it sends a message of gratitude and thoughtfulness. It's also more memorable. But I recommend buying a book of stamps to have ready to facilitate the old-fashioned gesture of sending a thank you card in the post. It's these little things that make a difference to your personal brand.

Digital networking

My company helps to rebrand senior executives when they are transitioning from one job to another. Part of this process is to help update their digital platforms to be used as tools for networking. Showcasing the best of you and your interests on LinkedIn, Facebook, Twitter and any other technologies is really important and there needs to be consistency across all of them. Make sure that your digital profiles are up to date, and share all relevant jobs, positions held, volunteer work, hobbies and information that others might find interesting. The more people know about you the better and the more contacts you will make. Knowledge is power and you'll have more opportunities to connect with a wider network.

Special tips for introverted, shy or socially anxious people

66 Quiet people have the loudest minds."

—*Stephen Hawking, English theoretical physicist*[14]

In my work I constantly meet with shy, introverted and anxious clients and I am privileged to listen to their stories. A number of these people feel obliged to become someone they are not. I have listened to people tell me they have felt pressured by their employers to overcome their shyness so they appear more confident. Some clients believe that to succeed in their careers they must be more outgoing and extroverted in order to be respected, noticed, recognized and promoted.

My belief has always been that we need confidence to succeed in life no matter what we choose to do. However, we live in a world that seems geared toward extroverts and this does not seem fair. Confident people like me who network with ease do not go through the agony that a large percentage of the population go through to talk to strangers.

Susan Cain's book *Quiet* has touched many people's lives and her TED Talk 'The Power of Introverts', where she talks about her own experiences as an introvert, is insightful. In her talk she says, 'a third of the universe are introverts so why are we wanting everyone to be the same?' Her talk has affirmed my views on the importance to accept people for who they are.

The definitions below of introverts, shyness and social anxiety have helped me to understand these important distinctions.

'Introverts ... may have strong social skills and enjoy parties and business meetings, but after a while wish they were home in their pyjamas. They prefer to devote their social energies to close friends, colleagues and family. They listen more than they talk, think before they speak and often feel as if they express themselves better in writing than in conversation. They tend to dislike conflict. Many have a horror of small talk but enjoy deep discussions.[15]

Shyness is the tendency to feel awkward, worried or tense during social encounters, especially with unfamiliar people. Severely shy people may have physical symptoms like blushing, sweating, a pounding heart or upset stomach; negative feelings about themselves; worries about how others view them and a tendency to withdraw from social interactions. Most people feel shy at least occasionally. Some people's shyness is so intense, however, that it can keep them from interacting with others even when they want or need to — leading to problems in relationships and at work.[16]

Social anxiety disorder, formerly referred to as social phobia, is an anxiety disorder characterized by overwhelming anxiety and excessive self-consciousness in everyday social situations. People with social anxiety disorder have a persistent, intense and chronic fear of being watched and judged by others and of being embarrassed or humiliated by their own actions. Their fear may be so severe that it interferes with work, school or other activities. While many people with social anxiety disorder recognize that their fear of being around people may be excessive or unreasonable, they are unable to overcome it. They often worry for days or weeks in advance of a dreaded situation. In addition, they often experience low self-esteem and depression.[17]

So what do you do if you really struggle in social situations?

- Rehearse while in your comfort zone. Practise 'networking' with relatives and friends. You probably mix with your friends and family every day. Maybe ask them questions that you would ask at a networking event to build your confidence. Remember that your friends were strangers to you once, and also take heart in knowing that a large percentage of people who are at networking events feel the same way as you.

- Try to remember names. When someone introduces themselves repeat their name back to them to help you memorize their name. It's a good technique that works. If the person's name is long or unusual, ask them if you are pronouncing it correctly.

- Ask other shy or introverted people what they do to manage their nerves at networking events and use any of their suggestions that you think will work well for you.

- Loose lips sink ships. Don't rely on alcohol to loosen up because you don't want to give a false impression of being gregarious and outgoing when that is not your personality.

- Be yourself. Don't feel pushed into being someone you are not.

- Start small. At the first event, have one meaningful conversation and slowly build on that; at the next event you might aim for two meaningful conversations.

- Don't set yourself up to fail. Don't have high expectations of yourself. Walk into an event and imagine that everyone else is like you (i.e. terrified to initiate a conversation!). Think about them and how you might help to support them. By focusing on the other person's needs it will distract you from your own insecurities.

- Accept risk. It is not going to always be easy. It's okay to make mistakes as this is the only way we learn.

- Talk about your hobbies rather than business. You are bound to find someone in the room who likes the things you do and shares your passions. Your job is to find them.

- There are meet-up groups all over the world where you can practise networking. Even joining a book club, a singing group or a language class will help you realize that your interpersonal skills are better than you think they are.

- Be sure to unwind. Take that time out for yourself. And also congratulate yourself after you have done well at a function you were dreading going to.

Our beliefs and our minds

66 Our beliefs control our bodies, our minds, and thus our lives ...”
—*Bruce H. Lipton, American biologist*[18]

I've worked with people who tell me that they are shy because someone once labelled them as shy, which they believed, and over time it became their truth. Your personal beliefs have a major impact on how you see yourself. Do you ever tell friends and colleagues that you hate networking? Do you tell yourself you are not good at working a room full of people you don't know? Is this really the truth or have you convinced yourself it is? A wise Buddhist teacher, Lama Yeshe, once said, 'Your bad is bad for you because your mind calls it bad.' This spiritual leader taught his students about the power of the mind and how it plays tricks on you. In my many years of teaching I have watched clients battle with their minds as they empower their negative thoughts to trick them into believing anything. Take it from a wise Lama: he urges consigning those negative thoughts to the garbage because they are not true and only have power if you believe them. They are your mind's version of 'fake news'!

Be careful not to label people (or yourself) and be aware of and empathetic with the limitations of others. Also, be careful not to live into the labels of 'shyness' or 'introvert' if that's what you've been told you are. Even clinical psychologists are wary of giving their clients a label, as it can influence the way a person thinks about themselves and can therefore limit or overly direct their behaviours.

Networking mistakes

Be careful to avoid the following pitfalls when networking:

- Going to a networking event unprepared and without an objective.
- Underestimating the importance of building and growing relationships face to face.
- Not talking to enough people at an event.
- Not getting to know people properly (for example, not asking enough questions).
- Talking about yourself too much or trying to sell a product rather than building friendships.

- Not using everyday etiquette and friendly body language.

- Not having a positive attitude and not thinking 'possibility'.

- Not following up with people or taking down contact details correctly.

- Not thanking the host and others who have referred new business to you.

- Not updating your digital platforms and not using them as tools when networking.

8

Styling your brand

> 66 Regardless of age, regardless of position, regardless of the business we happen to be in, all of us need to understand the importance of branding. We are CEOs of our own companies Me, Inc. To be in business today, our most important job is to be head marketer for the brand called you."
>
> —*Tom Peters, American writer on business management*[1]

If you want a good personal brand, you need to think about your visual identity as a whole. This means that there has to be a consistency throughout your entire offering which includes colours, logos, images, websites, social media, marketing collateral and appearance (including your clothing and personal styling). In this chapter we'll look at all of these elements.

When clients come to me, they buy into the Maggie Eyre brand. The styling of my brand reflects my personality. Some of the words people use to describe me are professional, unconventional, outgoing, warm, courageous and confident and my company values are based around these characteristics.

Colours

As I mentioned earlier, I love the colour orange. Sitting on my desk between the piles of papers is a vibrant, lacquered orange glasses case. Next to it are copies of my latest revised book, *Speak Easy*, standing upright with their orange spines, striking and shiny. Perched in a wooden stand next to my computer screen is a handful of black, orange and white business cards with my Fresh Eyre logo (that has been with me since the beginning) highlighted by the sun. These are the colours of my brand — orange, black and white — and they have been since the start of my company.

It's useful to research the meaning of colours, especially if you are still brainstorming your personal brand.

Many colour experts say that orange is the colour of joy and creativity and, together with my Fresh Eyre business associates, we embody both qualities when teaching our clients and in our workshops. For me, the adjectives which best reflect my feelings about the colour orange are 'extroverted' and 'uninhibited'. These are words my loved ones use to describe my personality and are words I, in turn, use to describe my principal trainers.

By now, you should know what your personal and professional values are, so find colours that speak to them. Write down your three top values and assign a colour to each and see if this helps you to decide on colours that suit your personal brand. Different colours mean different things to many of us. What is the first colour that you are consistently drawn to? What adjective would you use to describe it?

Brand brainstorming

66 100 per cent execution of a 20 per cent plan is better than 20 per cent execution of a 100 per cent plan. If you don't do anything then nothing will ever get done."

—Linus Sebastian, YouTube personality and founder of Linus Media Group[2]

When considering how to best represent your brand, there are numerous aspect to consider in order to ensure consistency in your styling. Let's now take a look at each of these.

The foundation

When building your brand, start right at the beginning. Building a clear foundation is really important because it will save you time and money in the long run. A fresh, creative approach is needed, which is why we pay experts to help us. Don't just settle for mediocre or easy; don't rush the planning stage and don't borrow or copy what everybody else is doing. Map it out step by step and start with the basics such as company name and domain name, which I talk about later in this chapter.

Be strategic

What does brand strategy mean and why is it important? American social media and branding expert Susan Gunelius says, 'Brand strategy is a long-term plan for the development of a successful brand in order to achieve goals.'[3] We all have goals, whether they are about fitness and health, or financial goals that will help determine your freedom and security. In these cases it pays to plan in order to help you reach your goal. It should be the same when establishing goals for your personal brand. Being strategic about your brand and having long-term goals gives you a path to follow so you don't go astray and get confused. Is your brand all over the place or is it consistent? Are you confident about the long-term plans for your career?

The only way to grow your personal brand (or company) and generate repeat business is to have a plan in place and stick to it. Think of it as having a book that has a very long shelf life. Without a publisher's plan, the editor's excellent work and the author's dedication to promoting that book, it would not be memorable and would go out of print. If you have a strong, clear visual identity that doesn't age, your clients will feel confident in you and you will feel confident marketing yourself.

With hard work and through devoting time and energy towards your goals, you will reach your destination. And remember to be a confident visionary of your own personal brand, because you know yourself better than anyone else.

> 66 Branding today is as much about consistently delivering on your promise as it is about differentiation. You have to position yourself in unique ways in order to stand out from others. You have to meet all of the subconscious expectations and go beyond the mundane to truly impress."
>
> —*Daniel Bliley, strategic marketing executive, University of Virginia*[4]

Standing out

What is it that is unique about your personal brand and what is it that is different about you? Customers and consumers are always looking for something that will give them something new and a little bit extra. You don't want to scare away new clients, but you do need to be seen, so don't be afraid to take a risk. After all, this is about being true to yourself and building a brand you are going to love and be proud of. You need to be inspired by everything visual because it's a bit like putting on a costume — it has to fit, it has to suit and it needs to be comfortable while standing out so people will look at it. Take care what you choose, because everything has a message.

Provocative Lady Gaga grabs attention in her outrageous outfits and has a strong personal brand. Whether you like her or not, she continues to surprise with a variety of outfits and music in keeping with the unique and unconventional brand she has created. Branding and marketing experts write about her being 'a master at personal branding'. She is an example of someone who goes beyond the mundane and people either love or hate her for it. The point is, everyone is noticing. This former Catholic girl was rebellious through her challenging and unhappy childhood with an alcoholic father and yet she found a creative way of expressing herself, defining a personal brand and moving away from the norm. Our past often shapes who we become as adults and we all find a way to survive and make something of our lives.

Go to professionals

Once you've decided on the brand elements, I recommend hiring professionals in graphic and web design to help you create a strong brand identify, as discussed in Chapter 4. Paying an expert will save you money in the long run, and it will also mean that you have consistency which exudes professionalism across all elements of your brand. There are things you can do on a low budget but be careful not to sabotage your brand in any way. You deserve to have a memorable personal brand that people are drawn to.

Just like buying an inexpensive jacket, you'll get what you pay for. The fabric will probably fade, fray at the edges, snag and fall apart in two years. But if you buy a quality jacket it will stand the test of time. I send clients to web companies that have a good track record with everything under one umbrella. Find a creative agency that provides graphic design, branding, marketing solutions, print and web services, and copywriting. You need your brand to get noticed and grow. Look at their clients, both small and large, to see how they have made a difference to these brands. This agency will look at your business goals, at any kind of inconsistent branding and your visual identity, and they will make changes to ensure that you are appealing to your target market. Make sure you are very involved with the process, as you know your brand better than anyone else. You could have the best design guru in the world, but they don't understand what you do, so work with your team to ensure the end result is quality. You must have a trusting relationship with anyone you hire.

Your company name

Many years ago, I was sitting in a café with a close friend when he had an 'a-ha' moment as we brainstormed ideas for the company I was forming. 'You should call this company Fresh Eyre,' said my friend Stuart Nash (Thanks Stu!), prompting me to leap from my chair, clapping with approval. I loved it straightaway because it included my Irish surname, which I am immensely proud of and attached to. I continue to this day to have a steady stream of complimentary feedback from clients about the name Fresh Eyre. The name of my previous company, Maggie Eyre Promotions, did not, by comparison, get a mention, a nod, a wink or a look-in. It was a perfectly reasonable and functional name, but in hindsight it was uninspired and forgettable. Now that I am 'Fresh Eyre', I get remembered. I also get unexpected attention, more business and, to seal the deal, lots of smiles and acknowledgment from people when hearing my company's creative and playful name. An added bonus is that no one will forget my surname.

When you're choosing your company name, run your ideas by a number of creative friends, particularly any who have a marketing background. Reach out far and wide for ideas and inspiration. When choosing a name for your company you need to think about what you want it to say. My recommendation is that you choose a name that is easy for people to remember but also has a snappy ring to it that directly relates to you.

Logos

I chose orange as the bright colour of my logo because it's bold and strong. It makes me feel good and it's a happy, positive colour. I chose a simple logo for a number of reasons. First of all, my monkey mind is busy, my life is frantic with juggling a million tasks and I need simplicity to ground me. I wanted to look at something simple that would remind me to slow down. My logo consists of two letters (f and e, standing for Fresh Eyre) with a square black backdrop. One letter is just breaking out of the square box. I like to think that this represents what I give my clients — permission to take leaps and bounds when they work with me and my talented trainers and not stay small and safe in their own square. The other way you could interpret my logo is the black box is night and the two orange letters represent the sunrise. You can interpret logos in lots of different ways.

When you design your own logo make sure it's about your personal expression. Think about the colour, the shapes and the size. After all, your personal brand is your story; it belongs to you and no one else.

Websites and social media

Personalizing your website and social media is important because your target market should know who you are, what you do and whether you are the kind of person who would work well with them, their staff or their team. It should be a perfect match.

When choosing images make sure they tell a story. The photographs I use on my website are of me in action, speaking to audiences or teaching workshops, because I want to illustrate my coaching style and the way I work. I like to think that new clients get to imagine themselves in the audience; I also hope they can immediately see I have an interactive approach, which is about people learning through doing.

Another good way to communicate what you do is to use videos. Take every opportunity to get your messages across to your audience. In my view, there's nothing more effective than a short film or video to describe more about your work. People will get to know you and it's more interesting than reading about you. Show us, don't tell us! Remember to post your videos on all of your digital platforms and link back to your website. This way, you will reach people that you never ever imagined, far and wide.

Your domain name

When you select a domain name for your website and social media platforms you should use the name of your company or something very close to it. This will ensure that your potential clients and target audience will recognize and remember you. Unfortunately, the name Fresh Eyre was taken so I used my full name maggieeyre.com, which is not a bad thing as my clients know my personal name more than my company name. Of course, it doesn't hurt having a well-known name from a book title — *Jane Eyre* — so shout out and humble thanks to the incomparable Charlotte Brontë!

Design

Your website needs to be easy to navigate. Your contact details should be easily visible and your services clear. People read very quickly and they want information fast, so don't make it hard work for anyone. By hiring experts you will have a well-designed, easy-to-use platform that works. Shop around, do your research, look at a range of digital design and marketing companies and their previous work and be sure to choose people you trust.

Consistency

Consistency means matching across your website and social medial platforms, which includes LinkedIn, Facebook, Twitter, Instagram and whatever other channels you use. Your logo, name, details, and copy should be consistent across all of these. This not only demonstrates professionalism, it tells people that you are organized and dependable. Consumers will trust you because your standards are high. You are telling people you are steady and reliable in your branding and this reflects the calibre of your work.

Marketing and collateral

66 Before you can decide on your brand fonts, colours or imagery, let alone your messaging, you need to know who you're trying to attract ..."
—*Amber Hurdle, brand strategist and author*[5]

All marketing material must be aligned with your brand. This means that there is a consistent theme running through every piece of stationery and correspondence. Whether it be hand-out materials or letterheads, corporate gifts or invoices, they all need to have the correct brand colours and logo so they communicate to your target audience what your company's brand is about. Children's birthday parties usually have a theme, so think of your brand as the perfect party portraying your personal brand. Everything matches and tells your story. For example, at the bottom of all proposals, evaluation forms, pre-course questionnaires, handouts and cover letters you will find my logo and contact details. I've always requested that orange is used somewhere on the covers or the spine of my books and I noted with pride that even the Indonesian version of *Speak Easy* came with orange artwork on the cover. In a photograph on the back of one of my books, I made sure that I was wearing an orange jacket with a black top. There are different shades of orange so it's crucial to get the right shade, especially if you use bright colours. This demonstrates to your target audience your professionalism, your attention to detail and that you care about the small things, which means you will care about them.

Clothing

66 Build a lifestyle around your brand and the audience will follow."

—*Eva Chen, former editor of* Lucky *fashion magazine*[6]

Does your clothing reflect your personal brand? If clothing has a language, what does yours say about you when you have a job interview, attend a board meeting or meet with your clients? What words would people use to describe your image? Stylish, professional, edgy, flamboyant, classical, funky, conservative, casual, smart or shabby and unprofessional?

An enjoyable part of my work is taking clients shopping and planning a suitable wardrobe for them. We are unfortunately, or fortunately, judged for what we wear. I suggest that you do an inventory of your wardrobe every six months and give away all the old, tired clothing you no longer wear unless they are one-off pieces and therefore precious. Ask yourself: When did I last wear this? Do I feel good in this? Why am

I keeping this jacket when it no longer fits me? Am I holding on to old memories? What does this garment say about me?

Pay attention to detail. Has that button been missing for two years off the bottom of the jacket? When was the last time you had your shoes polished and repaired? Do you pencil in a regular haircut? Are your chewed or chipped nails making you feel embarrassed? Will you feel more confident in clothes that make you look good and suit your body shape and personality?

People will remember your clothing more than you think. I personally feel proud when I have planned my wardrobe the week before an important meeting, presentation, client pitch or workshop. I also urge my team to think carefully about how they dress and they, in turn, understand how I want our clients to see us as a team of professionals in the business classroom. My company is all of us, not just me. We represent the Fresh Eyre brand but we all express our personalities differently through our clothing. We are all different shapes, sizes and heights but all think carefully about the clients when we are planning our clothing. If you have staff who need to 'scrub up', get them some help or support so they do not let your brand down.

You do not need to have a lot of money to look good. Over the years I have introduced many clients to quality second-hand stores where they pick up bargains including new top international brand clothing. I also encourage giving away your clothes to people who cannot afford expensive quality garments. This has been my practice and it gives me comfort knowing my clothing lives on in other people's lives, homes and workplaces.

Let me invite you into my wardrobe. The first thing you will see is a backdrop of black jackets, trousers, skirts and dresses. Sixty per cent of my wardrobe is black, 20 per cent is orange, 10 per cent white and the rest multicoloured. Of course, I've got other colours in my wardrobe like blues, greens and browns but I like to wear my brand colours when I am training. A senior businessman once beamed at me as I walked in the door on the second day of his training while quipping, 'Gosh, you're not wearing your brand colours today. Every time you work with me you're wearing black, white and a little bit of orange.' I was speechless that he had noticed my clothing and that it reflected my brand colours. It made me remember that clients and customers do notice these things.

Does your style stand out?

66 In order to be irreplaceable, one must be always different."
—*Coco Chanel, French designer*[7]

If you want to stand out, then wear something different. Statement clothing yells 'I am confident and bold and embrace who I am'.

I was born with bright ginger hair and a snow-white complexion, and I felt different from the time I could walk. Of course, I hated the way I looked because I was teased constantly and called cruel names like 'ginger nut'. It was humiliating that my long ginger ringlets attracted so much attention. But loathing turned to love and everything I detested about being one of the Celtic redheaded tribe became something I was immensely proud of as a young woman. Today, I still stand out with my orange hair and am grateful.

Celebrate your differences and never feel inferior about being different in a crowd. Be true to your own style and do not wear anything you feel silly or uncomfortable in.

Fashion

66 What you wear is how you present yourself to the world, especially today, when human contacts are so quick. Fashion is instant language."

—*Miuccia Prada, Italian fashion designer*[8]

Before I take any client shopping I ask the question, 'Do you have any concerns?' My clients often worry about the cost of buying smart, quality clothing. I also try to steer them away from fads in fashion. I make a point of talking about longevity and emphasize how 'being in fashion' is fine but trends come and go, and if you buy quality clothing you want to get your money's worth and keep on wearing what you love.

When I shop I never think about what's in fashion. Rather, I think about the following:

- Do I feel good in this clothing?
- Do I look attractive?
- Do I feel comfortable?
- Will I get good use out of this outfit?
- What do I have in my wardrobe at home that will work with this garment?

In 2003, I fell passionately in love, my nose pressed against a shop window, with a hot pink and black Versace woollen winter pencil skirt and stylish fitting jacket with a zipper to the neck. Next to this were tall leather boots with pink stitching at the sides and pink lining. My instant crush won the day and by the next week I was sitting up proud and straight, feeling uber-cool on the set of a morning TV program in my new outfit. I felt sensational and believed that the cost was worth it, even though I had to pay off the outfit over many months to the charming man who ran the shop. The suit was unusual and stood out, which I thought served a business purpose. These were the early days of promoting my book *Speak Easy* and I was fortunate to have six interview slots over as many weeks to talk about each chapter. I chose my clothing carefully for each appearance, so I felt confident.

If you are in the limelight (even for a short promotional period in your business) your clothing needs to reflect your brand, personality and the product you are selling or representing. I didn't buy this suit because it was a top brand; rather, I made the purchase because it suited my personality and I felt a million dollars in it. It matched the content of the book and my personal brand at the time.

Accessories

> ❝ The accessory should leave an impression that matches your brand and strengthens it, building your brand without overshadowing."
>
> —*Jacob Share, Israeli blogger and social media expert*[9]

Accessories are as important as clothes and provide an opportunity for you to say more about your personal brand by expressing yourself. Telling stories about your accessories is an interesting way of connecting with people and a good ice-breaker at events. When I admire someone's jewellery or scarf and he or she shares a story about it, I am more likely to remember that person. As a member of British royalty, the Duchess of Cambridge has access to the most dazzling jewellery collection on the planet and yet she's seen wearing inexpensive Zara costume jewellery necklaces now and then. This is savvy accessorizing and I think is probably calculated to send a message. Not only does she remind people of her roots but she says to the British people, 'I'm with you, approachable and down to earth.'

All of my jewellery has a story attached to it as, I'm certain, does yours. What I love about accessories like jewellery, bags, gloves, hats, headbands, shoes, socks, ties, tie clips, cuff links, scarves, shawls and glasses is that they can transform a look. A brooch can be the perfect conversation starter (and it's even cool to see men in suits wearing a brooch). I like to think that fashion has no rules and that anyone can feel confident enough to be expressive without judgment no matter what your gender or sexuality. Gifts from people I love and care about are some of my most treasured accessories and some go right back to my early adulthood. They reflect the story of my life.

Accessories: tips for women

Mix up your jewellery — layers look great.

Mix up colours and experiment with shapes.

Carrie from *Sex and the City* was right: shoes make a statement!

Find antique or meaningful stones and get something made up so you have an original piece.

Wear sentimental jewellery and tell its story as a reflection of who you are and where you come from.

Insure any expensive treasures. It always pays off.

Accessories: tips for men

Take your suits and shirts to the best drycleaners so they do not get damaged.

Express yourself through your socks — branch out.

If you wear a tie handkerchief, buy silk.

Bow ties are fun and not just for black-tie dinners.

> 66 Don't be into trends. Don't make fashion own you but you decide what you are, what you want to express by the way you dress and the way you live."
>
> —*Gianni Versace*[10]

Having an interest in fashion means I buy books about fashion and couture and, when I travel, I like to observe street fashion and snap away on my phone camera at people wearing cool and quirky items (with their permission, of course!). In cities like Milan and Paris, which I visit regularly, I'm always looking for inspiration for me and my clients. My belief is that your accessories are personal, so wear the accessories you like and that mean something to you — don't get caught up in fashion. And don't be afraid to be zany and show some flair. You are more likely to be remembered when you do.

What to avoid

- Clothes that don't fit properly, that are too tight or too big.
- Worn, frayed fabric.
- Ripped clothing (unless it's fashion jeans).
- Scuffed or unpolished shoes.
- Stained clothing.
- Chipped or dirty nails.
- Make-up on the inside of your collar.
- Dirty shirt cuffs.
- Un-clean hair.
- See-through clothes or anything inappropriate (dress for the occasion).

9

TED Talks: A tool in building your personal brand

> 66 The key part of the TED format is that we have humans connecting to humans in a direct and almost vulnerable way. You're on stage naked, so to speak. The talks that work best are the ones where people can really sense that humanity. The emotions, dreams, imagination."
>
> —*Chris Anderson, curator, TED[1]*

Sleep experts would say I have a bad habit. Apparently to get a good night's sleep you should not precede your sleep routine with too much screen time. But my little night-time pleasure is to be transported into the passions and purpose of people all around the world as they share their life's work and story through a TED Talk. When the speaker is captivating or the topic compelling, my eyes are glued to the screen and the clock ticks on well past my bedtime. TED Talks have become my adult equivalent of taking a torch to bed as a child and hiding under the bed covers to read a book in order to be transported into a new world of possibilities.

I have intentionally decided to dedicate a chapter to the cultural phenomenon that is TED Talks. Even if you don't expect to give a TED Talk anytime soon or it's not in the cards for you (although you never know!), I encourage you to read these pages carefully and apply the tips and techniques to any speech or presentation you give. This chapter is useful for everyone on the hunt for public speaking tips and tricks of the trade. I also urge, if you haven't yet done so, to observe TED Talk speakers online with the aim of gleaning ideas and inspiration from their styles and performances.

We can learn from people who have raised their profile on the digital TED Talk platform, where 800 million people worldwide have watched a plethora of talks in 100 languages from people of diverse cultural backgrounds. TED Talks have been a roaring success through combining the power of ideas, expressed in intimate and very real language and transmitted via new technologies. It's also a very refreshingly non-commercial enterprise, interested in human potential and not profit while aiming to shun elitism, sexism and racism. I am constantly reminding

TED organizers in my country to have equal gender representation on their stage. The first thing I do when the latest email from TED drops with the speakers' line-up is count the number of men to women speakers. Mostly they and their colleagues globally get it right. I even noticed when googling TEDwomen.com how a conference held in New Orleans in 2017 had a majority of presentations from women.

In researching the level of preparation speakers engage in before taking the TED stage, I have found that many set aside a rehearsal ratio of one hour for each minute of their speech. That's a lot of hours outside your day job. I like to share this information with my clients whether I am preparing them for a TED Talk or any sort of public speech, as it speaks to the level of commitment required to shine on the stage. You could be invited at some stage of your career to be on the TED podium, which, thanks to its credible reputation, would provide a great opportunity to build and grow your personal brand.

If you have never seen a TED Talk, do so today by visiting the site at www.ted.com. I see it as a healthy addiction, hobby or pastime, one that feeds your brain with stimulating ideas and knowledge.

Conceiving a cultural phenomenon

The first TED event was held in California in 1984 and brought together three speakers from three different industry sectors: technology, entertainment and design, thus the acronym TED. At first, the platform's success was modest but by the 1990s it began to find its feet, becoming a highly anticipated event for scientists, philosophers, business people, artists, philanthropists and many others. British journalist and entrepreneur Chris Anderson's non-profit Sapling Foundation acquired TED in 2001 and Anderson became its curator. He prescribed talks of precisely eighteen minutes, believing this is enough time to hold people's attention and say something that really matters, including on the internet. He says that shorter talks are acceptable but one must never run longer than eighteen minutes. From my experience of watching TED Talks and coaching people for this format, I think he is spot on in his thinking, as any longer and the audience loses focus.

With Anderson taking the TED platform non-profit, its name as a podium to seek and host the 'the most interesting people on Earth' under the slogan 'Ideas worth spreading' grew and the ideas and speeches that flowed from its events became much-discussed and debated around the globe. Thanks to clever use of developing technologies to spread the conference presentations, the talks and speakers who made them often went viral. These days, being invited to give a TED Talk is considered an honour as well as an opportunity to become an overnight sensation. Imagine your personal brand soaring in 24 hours and imagine potentially having half a million viewers in a day. It certainly makes all that hard work and preparation worth it! Today, TED conferences are staged in cities around the world, so if you are a leader or innovator in your field, taking the TED stage is available to you.

Why do a TED Talk?

" Stories are just data with a soul."

—Dr Brené Brown, PhD, research professor, University of Houston[2]

If you get an offer to make a TED Talk, grab it. The reasons are pretty obvious. It's a sure way to grow your personal brand and get your name out there into the public eye. It's also a great way to hone your public speaking skills and become more confident on a stage. Spreading the word about your latest research, work, creation or company's mission is also a bonus. You get free access to a live audience and have the opportunity to present on a digital world stage that sometimes gets millions of views. TED organizers provide coaching at no cost for those invited to speak, which I think is a very smart and generous idea. Not only does TED provide a podium to showcase people and their expertize and ideas, but it also equips them to feel confident and supported when they take the big step onto TED's centre stage.

Whatever your objective is, I acknowledge you if you are about to take the TED stage or have already done so. Well done for stepping up, making yourself vulnerable and doing something many people would shy away from through fear of failure. While it's a chance for you to get something, I also applaud what you are giving. This a forum of magnificent education and inspiration. The personal stories and hidden secrets revealed ask viewers to pause and ponder their own lives, and examine their own actions and goals. While we rely on great speeches with accurate data and information, we rely also on people sharing their deepest insights and even shame and fear in order to make a difference to who we are in the world both professionally and personally.

Why watch TED Talks?

For some people, listening to podcasts is a way to learn, re-imagine the world and sit with some big questions. For me, TED provides the same gift. I see it as my 'alone' time in which to grow while being inspired, moved and entertained. It's also a big part of my work so I can recommend memorable, worthy talks to clients and colleagues who are fossicking for inspirational and precious new material. After coaching many anxious, hand-wringing clients for their debut TED Talk, I have grown to respect this unique international organization, which allows so many to speak about and view transformative ideas. Sitting in the audience, I often feel like a proud yet anxious mum as they deliver their thoroughly rehearsed performances. I am ready with a warm post-speech hug and constructive, honest feedback. I have also spent hours in meetings with TED organizers who have hired me as a coach so we are all on the same page about what makes a good TED Talk. Timing and good content is essential and the rehearsals that organizers require help you to stick to the strict time frame.

A client of mine has given permission to share an email she wrote to me after her TED Talk in 2015. I like to say she went from zero to hero throughout the process.

———————————————— 99 ————————————————

I see the TED experience as life-changing. I learnt a number of things about public speaking but most importantly I learnt to honour my life experiences and pain. Quite unexpectedly, I have never felt I would feel relieved by opening up my personal life pages and offering those pages for others to read. I didn't realize that the untold heavily guarded stories on those pages weaved with my research would bring tears for members in the audience and that students and colleagues would walk up to me and say that what I shared had struck a chord with them and inspired them! I now try to bring my spirit to public speaking rather than leaving it behind in order to fit into some set template of what is expected in public speaking.[3]

Qualifying for the TED stage

Each presenter is given a thorough brief in a carefully written document. Speakers are advised, 'You do not need to be the world's foremost expert on the topic, but you have to be an expert.'[4]

I have stunned a few people at the end of a presentation coaching class by declaring with total confidence, 'I think you should do a TED

Talk'. The usual response is, 'Are you kidding me?' But I never am. Because worthy ideas and/or interesting data combined with personal stories qualify you to be a TED candidate. I also have some clients who whisper in my ear, 'One day I want to give a TED Talk' and, for many, that's a fantastic and attainable goal for us to roll up our sleeves and work towards.

My favourite TED Talks are often related to my work in some way, so I enjoyed American psychologist Amy Cuddy's talk on body language. Her personal brand is strong and you cannot help but be moved by her story of recovering from a car accident. I am also a huge fan of Brené Brown's ground-breaking research on shame and vulnerability. Her stunning TED debut in 2011 is essential viewing.

If you are concerned about the environment (like most of us), you might watch Al Gore's TED Talks in 2006 and ten years later in 2016. Or if it's savvy tips from a successful businessman who has his own stellar personal brand you're after, look for Sir Richard Branson's interview on the TED couch with Chris Anderson from 2007. His Holiness Pope Francis spoke from the Vatican in April 2015, participating on the TED stage on a gigantic screen. His talk is good, and he comes across as authentic.

There's one strict rule in TED Talks: no promoting your business. In my view, this contributes to the popularity and unique branding of TED Talks. Pope Francis, in a canny performance, doesn't promote the Catholic church in his talk but he does talk about world peace and climate change. It's worth watching even if you are not Catholic.

I support clients all the way when rehearsing for a TED Talk, especially during the moment when they push a panic button and begin to melt down over the impending talk, vowing to cancel, run and abandon ship! Most of us, at some stage in our lives, let fear strangle our dreams and taunt us when we stumble and lose confidence. My job is to make sure clients believe they can do it, fear or no fear.

Getting through the TED door

There isn't any one way to receive an offer to deliver a TED Talk. So how do you get invited?

In my experience, and through speaking to friends and colleagues (some of whom have graced the TED stage), one way is to simply pick up the phone, call the TED office in your city or country and invite the organizer to see you in action when you next speak. Alternatively, you could send some video of your work. You could also set up a meeting with your local TED organizer and share your story in a conversational way, or ask someone who you trust and who values you to do it on your behalf. Many big TED sponsors, like universities, will make it possible for their professors or senior academics to be speakers as part of the sponsorship package. (Universities are obvious sponsors, as their prime focus is education.) There has to be something in it for the sponsors (apart from publicity on the day) in order for them to get good value from seeing their experts sharing their work on the TED stage. Remember this if you are looking for a person or an entity to back your TED goals. I have often picked up the phone or sent an email recommending a potential speaker for TED because I know how the organizers are scouting about in the community and are always on the lookout for new speakers. So don't be shy.

Do you want to take the stage, or can you think of someone who would be a dynamic TED speaker? Maybe you could make someone else's dream come true or, at the very least, make sure an inspirational story from your community gets the attention it deserves. Some stories need to be dragged into the light, and when they are, they shine and illuminate communities, countries and sometimes the world.

> **"** At the end of my life, I want to be able to say
> I contributed more than I criticized."
>
> —*Dr Brené Brown, research professor, University of Houston*[5]

What makes a good TED Talk?

You've made the decision, contacted your local organizer and secured your first appearance as a TED speaker. Now it's time to prepare! So what makes for a good TED Talk, one that will engage the audience and be remembered? Here are some tips.

- Know your material. Don't look too much at the autocue or your notes. The odd glance is fine, but memorizing your talk is preferable and makes an impact.

- Be authentic, someone who is real and being themselves.

- Make sure your talk has a good structure and clear messages.

- Don't use jargon. Use everyday language and avoid technical words.

- Have a memorable story.

- Aim to include spontaneous natural gestures, which personalize and show expression.

- Use relatable examples.

- A strong introduction is compelling, so make sure you give some thought to this part of your talk.

- Use clear slides, images and photos (not too many).

- A well-rehearsed TED Talk will be more memorable (you cannot rehearse too much).

" Build your speech from an emotional place rather than from the content."

—*Kristi Hedges, American leadership coach and author*[6]

Allie Webber, a senior trainer at Fresh Eyre and great friend, is, like me, a devotee of TED Talks. For this chapter, I sought her expertise and asked her to choose and critique a recent TED presentation and share why it works. I have also added my thoughts at the end. Our thinking is that if you, too, watch the speaker and then read our notes and feedback, it might be useful should you be asked to write and present either a TED Talk or another type of important speech.

Here's what Allie had to say:

———————————————— 99 ————————————————

Like Maggie, I love TED Talks and find them a great way to learn about love, life, the universe and everything. I also find them a great way to learn more about the art of storytelling. Content is my part of the magic we provide in training so I'm always fascinated in how people tell their stories and spark conversation about great ideas, what are the devices they use, what works and why.

Beth Malone was selected for the TED Residency program in 2017. She describes herself as an artist, connector, consultant, educator/teacher, entrepreneur, explorer, world traveller, writer and editor. She is passionate about art, writing, trips on planes, her family, dementia, end-of-life care, surfing, trucks, reading, walking, yoga, talking and old folks. Beth is the founding executive director of Dashboard, an organization that's presented award-winning exhibitions in cities around the United States including Atlanta, New Orleans, New York and Detroit.

Beth's talk is called 'How my dad's dementia changed my idea of death (and life)' and you can view it here: www.ted.com/talks/beth_malone_ how_my_dad_s_dementia_changed_my_idea_of_death_and_life.

Posted to the TED website in June 2017, at the time of writing it had been viewed over 1 million times.

Having lived in and around dementia with some of my nearest and dearest (my mother and grandmother), I really relate to the tragedy, overwhelming sadness and humour of this story. It is simple, powerful and has a really strong message. This is a comparatively short TED Talk but works beautifully.

Beth is brave enough to share part of the devastating and dramatic story of her father's journey with dementia. She uses an attention-grabbing opening: 'I've been doing some thinking: I'm going to kill Dad.' Then, there's good use of repetition as she repeats her intention to kill her father who has frontotemporal dementia (FTD). She then explains why she wants to take this extreme action and returns to her theme as she discusses the idea with her sister, finally recovering her sanity and sense of humour.

Another selling point for the talk is simple language that's easy to connect with and remember. For example: 'My dad's been really sick for a decade. Three years ago, we had to move him out of the house, the house that I grew up in, the house that he built with his own hands … My strapping, cool dad with the falsetto singing voice had to move into a facility with round-the-clock care when he was just 65.'

I watched Beth's TED Talk and was very moved by her sincerity. Beth has great presence and is unafraid to show her emotion. It's powerful and touching. This is a woman who has had a direct experience with dementia, so is now an authority to speak about this crippling disease from watching her dad decline. I have no one in my family with dementia but would recommend anyone watch this TED Talk. It's heartfelt and gripping. Her language shows you rather than just tells you. It doesn't feel over-rehearsed and she is unafraid to share her suffering, desperation and the sheer torment of being a daughter yearning for a father whose body is there but whose mind is not. She effectively communicates the struggle that any child would go through and the drastic action she plays out in her mind to ease her dad's suffering and that of her family. If she were in my class I would say, 'Well done Beth for your courage!'

> 66 Great communications reach your head and touch your heart. Most people who deliver a presentation forget the 'heart'."
>
> —*Carmine Gallo, American author of* Talk Like TED[7]

Tips for a good TED Talk

- Read the official TEDx Speaker Guide thoroughly.
- Read Carmine Gallo's book *Talk Like TED*.
- Rehearse often, and way in advance, with an experienced presentation coach or a trained actor.
- Make sure every rehearsal is filmed and played back so you can get critiqued and learn.

- Reassure your coach you are 100 per cent committed and come to each session having done your homework.

- Mark out a large circle on the floor using the same measurements as the circular red carpet used in TED Talks. Work out any movement.

- Rehearse with a professionally qualified voice coach.

- Do a vocal warm-up before each rehearsal.

- Practise your speech with a timer or use your smartphone stopwatch.

- Practise with an autocue well before your TED Talk if you choose to use it.

- Watch other TED Talks and observe body language and listen to passionate voices.

- Eat healthy food and get plenty of sleep in the week leading up to your TED Talk.

- Stay hydrated by drinking enough water and avoid alcohol the week before.

- A TED Talk audience is supportive, so remember they are on your side.

- Be clear about what you want your audience to walk away with.

- Believe in yourself.

---

66 Our life is frittered away by detail. Simplify, simplify."

—*Henry David Thoreau, American essayist and philosopher*[8]

Things to avoid

Here are some pitfalls to avoid when planning and delivering your TED Talk:

- Beware of adding too much detail in your talk.

- Avoid putting your speech notes in your slides (this goes for all presentations).

- When using slides make sure they emphasise a point or are relevant.

- Don't try to be someone else. Be yourself.

- Don't go over time (I saw this happen once with a young man and the audience was embarrassed for the speaker. The MC had to rescue the situation).

- Don't overkill with statistics.

- Be careful to avoid a weak start to your speech. Watch successful TED Talks and note how they begin.

- Don't include too much technical jargon or terminology.

- Do not pitch a product or sell in any way (this is a strict TED rule).

- Bad lighting is out of your control but always do your research and check out previous filming at that centre or community TED venue.

What to wear for a TED Talk

Wear clothing you feel comfortable in and that you like, but also think about your personal brand. If you are a fashion designer wear something that shows off your designs or creativity. If you work in advertising wear jeans, a cool T-shirt and a jacket. A high-profile former mayor and surfer I admire walked onto the stage in bare feet and his trousers rolled up. His stories about his childhood at the beach and his surfing days matched his clothing. It was memorable and a perfect fit for his TED Talk.

The worst thing you can do is wear a suit if you only wear one once or twice a year. This is not a wedding or a funeral, it's a TED Talk that will be seen on the internet and observed as a one-off performance on a large stage. Wearing something you do not normally wear would be inauthentic. TED Talks connect with a live and digital audience and for that to happen authentically, you have to be real. However, you can get very hot on a stage under the lights, so think carefully about your clothing as the last thing you want to do is sweat profusely!

I persuade my female clients to wear make-up and I hire a professional make-up artist (and hairdresser all in one) for the morning of the TED event. Your face can look shiny under the lights, so men also need to at least wear powder on the day. I also urge men to go to the hairdresser or barber the day before or, better still, make an appointment on the morning of your talk.

Amy Cuddy's TED Global talk in 2012 is the second most viewed TED Talk (the first being Ken Robinson's on 'Are our schools killing creativity?'). Cuddy, a highly respected professor at Harvard University, bought an expensive Fendi dress a few days before her TED appearance, having agonized over her clothing choice for the occasion. However, a few days before the talk she questioned why she was planning to dress so unlike her usual self. So Cuddy ditched the Fendi and chose instead to wear an emerald green top with a silver choker necklace, a short fitted skirt and long draped jacket. She wore what she felt comfortable in and what suited her, which is what I advise all my clients to do, whether taking the TED stage or any other.

Clothing tips for TED Talks

Note that the same rules apply for television appearances.

- No stripes or checks (they can strobe or distort camera lenses).
- No white clothing.
- No (all) black clothing.
- Avoid long, dangling earrings.
- Look smart and tidy.
- Reflect your personality in your clothing.
- Think about your target audience.

10

Leadership in the limelight

Not for many generations has the world been so anxious and, in so being, many of its citizens have been galvanized to take action and engage. People are worried, frightened, polarized and angry about what is happening to our planet and its climate. There is concern over the policies of world powers such as the United States, Russia and China, the antics of global leaders and their attacks on institutions such as a free press and the United Nations; and again we are facing the threat of nuclear proliferation and war. As a human race, we are in turmoil over the rise of extremist and radical hate speech embodied in groups and political forces that support them. We are in disarray over refugees, people-smuggling and human slavery, as well as the continuing struggle to combat inequality and abuse based on race or gender. Supporters on all sides of these arguments yell and at each other without, it often seems, a steadying hand to guide us towards solution and resolution. The list of global challenges and red flags is so long that sometimes I, an eternal optimist, find myself suspended in a moment of despair as a global citizen who is alarmed by the intersection in which we find ourselves in the 21st century. I suggest that this is the time, once again, for voices to be raised and for engagement. This is the time for civic action and service. This is the time to think about a leadership role, running for office at whatever level of government you feel comfortable. If you already hold office, then this is your greatest hour because we especially need strong, decisive and honourable stewardship right now in our governments and institutions.

I have trained, supported and invested in elected officials for more than 25 years. I have worked with prime ministers, opposition leaders, public leaders and council members — in total, a whole bag of brave and civic-minded people who step up to the plate to represent and protect us as they see fit. Many argue that, just like in the 1960s and 1970s, the world finds itself again on a fault line. So much is rumbling and shaking and, as I write, there are deep concerns about which way our planet will go, both ecologically and geopolitically. It was former United States President Theodore Roosevelt who spoke the following rousing words more than a century ago.

66 The credit belongs to the man who is actually in the arena, whose face is marred by dust and sweat and blood; who strives valiantly; who errs, who comes short again and again."
—*Theodore Roosevelt, President of the United States, 1901–09*[1]

For those of you thinking of getting into the arena or if you are already in there, this is a chapter for you. I have learnt a lot in the decades working with leaders in the public eye, so I want to share and dedicate my knowledge and know-how with gratitude for your current or impending service. Thank you. We need you.

Holders of public office receive saturated media attention and scrutiny, which brings into acute focus the fundamentals of building, maintaining and protecting a brand. It's my professional opinion that the very same principles that apply to leaders in corporate, academic and non-government organizations apply to those who run for public office. If you aspire to one day be prime minister, president, a member of parliament, councillor, head of state, chief of staff or a leader in any space for that matter, or if your career relies on campaigning for votes or lobbying to achieve an outcome, then the following pages will help you reinvent and protect your personal brand. Equally, if you serve as a minder, a confidant, a press secretary, a personal assistant or advisor, this chapter will add to your tip sheet to protect and grow the personal brand of your boss. It will also give insight into how I work with such leaders and aspiring leaders, and in showing you my work practices I hope you will gain some ideas for how to be your own coach in fostering and protecting your personal brand.

Looking after your reputation is paramount when you are a leader who either seeks to build trust with people and to improve their lives in safe, thriving communities, or to responsibly grow corporations. You need a toolkit to build your brand and keep it honest. If you are studying politics at university, lecturing in public policy or interested in leading a campaign for a political party, your knowledge about personal branding will educate your students and followers and keep you focused on the crucial point of brand awareness and protection.

Service and sacrifice

> " Each time you stand up for an ideal, you
> send forth a tiny ripple of hope."
> —*Robert Kennedy, former US Attorney General*[2]

Any personal brand, whether it be political, corporate or academic, encompasses clothing and appearance, body language, voice and messaging. From the beginning of any high-profile public career, massive sacrifices are made. From what I have personally seen and experienced, a career in the spotlight guarantees that every misstep and out-of-place word is commented on and often weaponized against you. Candidates and up-and-coming leaders can work endless voluntary hours without income or acknowledgment, fighting for causes about which they are passionate and there is no guarantee that this work will bear fruit when voters decide your fate. Deciding to run for office or a public leadership position requires you and those around you to buckle up for a very bumpy ride along an often booby-trapped obstacle course.

People in the public eye can be criticized every second of the day all over the world. They are ripped apart by their opposition in parliament, dissected in the media and by the general public, spat on in the street by angry protesters, yelled at on the campaign trail and in extreme cases murdered by hateful, disturbed members of the public. A tragic example was the death of British Labour politician, Jo Cox, who was shot and stabbed in 2016 in her constituency in Batley, Yorkshire, England. It was the first murder of a British politician since 1990, when Ian Gown was assassinated by the IRA.

When Jo was killed on 16 June 2016, it was a sad and shocking reminder to me of the inherent vulnerability facing people who choose to serve in public life. Jo Cox's life ended after she simply walked along the street on her way to a meeting with her constituents. Her husband, Brendan Cox, eulogized his late wife in a way that transcends political persuasion and touched the hearts of people from all parties. 'Jo's killing was political ... What a beautiful irony it is that an act designed to advance hatred has instead generated such an outpouring of love. Jo lived for her beliefs, and on Thursday she died for them, and for the rest of our lives we will fight for them in her name.'[3]

While this is an extreme example of sacrifice through service, life as an elected official will inevitably see your personal brand take a series of very hard knocks. All the politicians and celebrities I know accept this as part of the job, although through my work I see the toll it takes on them and their partners. A sense of humour is certainly required if you are going to stay sane because it's a bruising and brutal environment, especially if your pure intention is public service. Staying true to your values and making a difference for the people and constituents you serve often gets lost in the cacophony of insults, name-calling and deliberate stunts that opposing factions and media generate to put you off your game. You need a strategy to keep you on-message and remind you of why you are serving, because there will be countless moments in every week that tempt you away from your mission and into defence mode.

I watched a senior minister, who is still my dear friend, suffer from stress, depression and anxiety as she contemplated abandoning public service, even though at the time her progressive female voice was unique and ground-breaking. She was being bullied by her boss, the Prime Minister, because she would not compromise her values, so she crossed the floor and brought down his government. Her actions changed the geopolitical arrangements of her country, New Zealand, and its relationship with the United States, and paved the way for New Zealand's now sacrosanct nuclear-free stance, enshrined in legislation. I salute her to this day for her courage. She made such an enormous contribution both nationally and internationally, and although it was unintentional, she managed to invent a well-respected personal brand for herself, based on values and independent politics, that inspired others to follow her example.

The lesson here is, yes, it will get tough. Excruciating, in fact. You might want to quit. But you need to find a way to reconnect with the simple and noble call of your original mission based on personal values. And sometimes that means finding a trusted person or team who can help you find your way back to believing rather than bolting.

The brief

When a client's 'team' gets in touch, usually through a media advisor, to ask me to consider working with him/her, typical concerns raised in their brief include:

- 'We need you to help us humanize him/her and help this leader to be more relatable.'
- 'We need you to coach him/her to smile and open up more.'
- 'We need him/her to look less serious and more relaxed on television.'
- 'We need you to work on wardrobe and style so the public identify with him/her.'
- 'We need you to build up confidence.'
- 'We want you to help him/her have more authority.'

If I were to weave together all of my briefing notes (which would add up to tens of thousands of words and comments), in the end they could be summarised in two words: personal confidence. My job is to build that while helping strengthen the client's personal brand, whose roots lie in the values and beliefs that inspired a run for office in the first place. Any public leader needs the public to get to know them as a real person and the vehicle for that is conventional media (TV, radio and print) as well as social media. The public also deserves to know the person, in my opinion, because casting a vote for someone is about the ideas they hold which, after all, have been shaped by their personal story and background. We cannot be expected to vote for people we do not know much about, and only through getting to know them will they gain our trust and earn our vote.

The audit

Research, study, rehearsal and insightful character analysis are the tools to help you perform best in any work arena or on any stage. In-depth and relentless research is how I begin on the path to understanding who any new client is, in this case, an already-elected official or candidate for office. I wade through endless interviews, both international and local, studying social media sites, listening to radio interviews and looking at print and television media. Forming my own impressions and opinions and coming up with ideas before I design a program is essential in achieving the best outcomes for my client. This is my concentrated homework time to examine, investigate and analyse why the public are not relating or responding to the leader I am about to work with. My advice to you is to set aside enough hours when researching your client's personal brands and apply any skills in this chapter to get to know people before or as you work with them.

I create a sort of storyboard, both visually and mentally, using photos from newspapers, magazines and online portals and pose the following questions in an exploratory session with myself:

- What is their posture saying?
- Does he/she look at ease or nervous?
- Is this a strained smile or one that speaks to me as real?
- Does their clothing impress or distress? Does his/her style suit or detract?
- Does their hairstyle help or hinder their image as a leader?

What I am looking for and asking is the following key question: 'Is she/he authentic?' Think about leaders who inspire and motivate you, and ask these same questions about them in order to figure out what helps them be successful.

The classroom

The classroom could be a private room in parliament, council chambers, a colleague's house, a politician's home or a secure hired venue away from prying eyes. The first day I walk into a client's office or home is the most important time. This meeting determines the beginning of a professional relationship based on trust and it's set up with an intention. The advisor will say something like, 'See if you both get on and click'.

I always go to the first 'meet and greet' with no expectations and an open willingness to build rapport.

What I am looking for, in return, is a dedicated commitment to hard work. I describe to my client the theatre-based methodology I use in my work. I explain that all our sessions will be experiential, not experimental. I tell them, 'There will be lots of creative improvisation exercises and loud, expressive movement and voice. At times, you will feel embarrassed and utterly out of your comfort zone. And that's okay. But if you trust me, this approach will work. I promise you, you are in a safe pair of hands. What the exercises will do is help you to be more spontaneous and relaxed and ad-lib when you need to. What I am giving you is an actor's toolkit to take away.' In this initial meeting, I listen and ask many questions to make sure my client is willing to enter into a personal branding program. 'What I care about is your reputation and how people perceive you,' I tell them.

There are five people in the training room: my camera operator, a senior and highly qualified journalist from my team, the media advisor, the client and myself. When our work begins, the atmosphere is still and quiet. This is an intense and organized presentation session that is carefully designed to increase the client's self-confidence. We review previous television or social media footage from the last few months and I critique the client's performance, starting with body language and voice. Self-critiquing one's presentation is a part of the learning process that I encourage in clients and in you. The typical questions I ask are, 'What do you think of your performance? What are you satisfied with? What's missing, in your view? Where would you like to improve?' When this self-review process is finished, we get into action with relaxing the body and the voice.

Relaxing your body

I invite the client to follow me with my movements to loosen their body. Bending my waist, I allow my arms to fall down over my head, almost touching the floor. Then I stand up straight, flapping and letting my legs and arms move while turning and swirling my feet in repetitive circles. I lift and drop my shoulders, moving my hips in hula hoop circles, shaking my buttocks while opening my mouth wide. I screw my face up tightly saying, 'crinkle your face like a prune' and stretch high toward the ceiling. My client imitates me, at first reluctant and very resistant, but gradually the inhibition gives way to ease. I assure them they are in a safe environment and in following these relaxation movements, they will feel energized and fully awakened.

Voice drills

66 It took me quite a long time to develop a voice, and now that I have it, I am not going to be silent."

—*Madeleine Albright, US Secretary of State, 1997–2001*[4]

An audience wants to be inspired by a visionary and to hear passion in their voice. Sounding passionate is about your enthusiasm for the ideas you are talking about and your voice reflects your thoughts and feelings. Technique is not as important as you might think. Leaders are not (in most cases) trained actors who have spent years ensuring their voice has a larger pitch range than most people. I encourage all the clients I work with to remember this from the outset and have realistic expectations and goals around their voice and delivery. But I share with them the basics in a thespian's vocal toolkit. If you want to project your voice and be heard at the back of a room you need to have a relaxed body. If you're tense it will be detected in your voice. When someone is tired it shows in their voice because it becomes flat and lacks highs and lows, variation of pitch, shade and colour.

As American voice legend Kristin Linklater (one of my gurus) says, 'To free the voice is to free the person'.[5] Sharing my knowledge from my days in the theatre is part of my practice when teaching and, thus, I insist on starting with a vocal warm-up. Some people tell me they feel a little uncomfortable at first but most find the vocal warm-up liberating and relaxing. Getting the blood flowing and endorphins racing to the brain makes us all feel instantly more energized.

Diction

When my team from Fresh Eyre works with a client, our camera operator, who also happens to be a talented actress and playwright, helps me in the noble art of voice coaching. Among the exercises we employ are tongue twisters like 'Unique New York, Unique New York' and 'around the rugged rocks the ragged rascal ran'. We explain as we go along why we are doing this and the value of clear diction. Diction exercises help us to enunciate words clearly and good articulation means pronouncing vowels and consonants. An audience needs to be able to hear the words so they perfectly understand the message and, in so doing, perceive the speaker as clear and confident.

Breath

I move my lips to make a sound like rumbling 'horse lips' in a theatre exercise called 'The Trill' where you blow air out through the mouth. Out of the corner of my eyes, I can often catch the client's media adviser smiling as they see the boss squirming in the initial attempts to imitate horse lips. But I keep going and then transition into a yoga breathing exercise to manage the nerves and relax the body. I demonstrate by raising my arms while taking in a deep breath, holding the arms above my head and releasing the air through my nose as my relaxed arms gently drop down in front of me to the side of my body. I remind my clients of the importance of breathing from the diaphragm and not the upper chest. Most see the value of these exercises immediately and don't feel embarrassed or shy.

The rehearsal: practice

" The work of rehearsal is looking for meaning
and then making it meaningful"

—*Peter Brook, English director and producer*[6]

'Standing by — action!' The camera rolls and we practise a twenty-minute speech for an upcoming event that the media advisor has pre-planned with me. The client reads the introduction, then inevitably pauses before stopping and apologizing as it's likely the first time they have seen the script. I'm ready for this scenario as I am familiar with the gruelling schedules most high-profile leaders have. Generally, there has been little or no time to read through any important speech before our session. And that's okay.

'Just start at the beginning, taking your eyes off the page as much as you can and we will play it back in ten minutes,' I tell my client. I put my hands on my cheeks and mould a smile on my face, reinforcing the message about being warm. The exercise is repeated until the lines are learnt, so that sense and meaning come through more in the delivery. I then involve the client in a self-critiquing exercise as we watch the video back. 'What do you see?' I ask. Responses can range from:

- 'I look stilted and my head's down too much.'

- 'My voice is fading away at the end of sentences.'

- 'My eyes look blank and it seems I don't believe in what I am saying.'
- 'My eyes are not relaxed and focused, which makes it seem like I don't believe my own words.'

There are so many different observations when someone self-critiques in a safe place. We work our way through the speech, filming as we go, and I encourage my client to ad-lib and use more everyday language. Being word-perfect is not the goal. Our journalist on the team, who is the content trainer, chips in with valuable constructive feedback about 'painting more pictures and telling more stories'. I stress the importance of pausing and slowing down the pace.

What I am looking for is a natural delivery rather than a polished performance, and in any speech you give this should be your aim, too.

The Unexpected

66 If you set out to be liked you would be prepared to compromise on anything at any time, and you would achieve nothing."
—*Margaret Thatcher, British Prime Minister, 1979–90*[7]

Inevitably, your personal brand will take a hard knock at some stage and this is something most politicians and leaders accept as part of the job. Not taking yourself too seriously is required if you are going to survive in a career of public service.

It was a particularly stinking hot public holiday in February 2016 in my country, New Zealand. The country's Minister of Economic Development, Steven Joyce, was out and about and holding a press conference when a rather large rubber pink dildo ricocheted through the air to wallop him on the nose. On cue it found its way into the frames of every TV and stills camera in attendance. 'That's for raping our sovereignty,' yelled a female protester who was angry at the Trans-Pacific Partnership (TPP) trade agreement. The video footage was played and re-played on national television and picked up by comedic presenter John Oliver on his show *Last Week Tonight*, who delighted in calling the incident 'Dildo-gate'. I am no prude so confess to having had a hearty giggle alone watching the news that evening. I suspected it would go viral, which was a great achievement for the protestor who grabbed the world's attention, probably unwittingly. On television I have seen eggs, flour, paint and mud thrown at politicians, but I have to say, never a sex toy. No media trainer in the universe is going to prepare a public leader for an incident like that. Steven Joyce managed his situation as well as he could, telling the media it was, 'a little bit humorous at the end of the day'. Often, it's best to move on by joining in with the laughter.

Alan Joyce, the chief executive of Qantas Airlines, was only three minutes into his speech at the West Business 'Leadership Matters' conference in Perth when an unknown man crept up behind him and confidently smacked a cream pie in his face. It's not every day you have to clean up your face and suit in front of 500 people. With a sense of humour, he came out with 'I don't know what that was about'. He stepped off the stage for a moment and cleaned himself off before returning and joking to the audience, 'Now, if there are any more pies, can you get it over with now?'

Why do it?

Every job has its limitations, downfalls and risks but most of us do not have our dirty laundry aired on prime-time television let alone become subjected to flying objects that should stay in the bedroom. You may be wondering why any intelligent person would choose a career in public office or in the public eye, given their most embarrassing moments and proverbial falls are parodied and made into comedy fodder.

Sacrificing your freedom and privacy for others is no easy feat and something most of us don't think about. When I was young, my attitude toward any high-profile person who was the target of this kind of behaviour was 'tough!' and I would say under my breath, 'suck it up, you chose this career'. Then I had a great deal of media exposure in various times in my life and got to experience the lows when I was judged or made fun of at my own expense. Now I choose to respect the risk-takers who stand up for the rights of others. Some of my dearest friends and clients work or have worked and served in the public eye. They are some of the most courageous and generous people I know. They simply want to make a difference in the world. Against all odds, they continue to stand by their values to help others live a better life. We choose leaders, pioneers and trailblazers to be our voice. And we have high expectations of the leaders we vote for. It's an important role, which is why nurturing and caring for your personal brand as a public figure is vital to the core.

I am privileged to have had the opportunity to work and fraternize with leaders at opposite ends of the globe since the 1980s. Although former US President Bill Clinton is a politician with a damaged personal brand, there was much in his style and approach that impressed me when I sat opposite him at a national fundraising dinner in 2003. I was expecting Clinton to just talk to the people on either side of him. I was pleasantly surprised at how informal he was as he made his way around the table, engaging in a meaningful conversation with every one of us. It was obvious to me that he had done his homework and had researched every dinner guest at the table. He was a big hit, not because he was Bill Clinton, but because he was so approachable and available for conversation with anyone about anything. Talking with him was like chatting to my neighbour across the fence. I observed him socializing and how he made every person feel special. His brand was likeable even though his tarnished reputation preceded him. Such inclusive behaviour goes a long way towards enhancing your personal brand, and is something I recommend you take note of for yourself.

Media

People in public leadership positions rely on the media to get their messages out there, but the media can often be cruel, so it's a mission filled with challenges. Most people never get to have a personal or private conversation with a renowned leader so they rely on what they see on television, hear on the radio or read in print or online. As a prominent leader, your media platform is your link to your audience. This is why it's important for politicians, business and educational leaders or anyone in a decision-making role to think about their personal brand in relation to the media, both digital and face-to-face.

If a journalist writes a great story about you, you are ecstatic. But if a journalist writes a negative story, it's disappointing. Don't retaliate and don't take it too personally. The majority of journalists deal with facts but sometimes things go wrong and they can misinterpret something you've said or gather information from an unreliable source. I've been misrepresented in the media a number of times in my career and it's distressing. Certain quoted sentences have stared back at me on the page when I didn't say them. But I have learnt over time to not attach so much meaning to the words that were inaccurate. Instead, I focus on creating a working relationship with that journalist because I need the media to promote my work. Of course, you'll need to stand up for yourself if the story is inaccurate to the point that it may damage your reputation in some way, but just remember that journalists are links to your voters or shareholders and you need them.

Journalists have a job to do and, for the most part, they do it well while sometimes erring, which is natural and human. While we need professional journalists to keep leaders honest, today we face increasing challenges because of the rise in what is called fake news. A good example of this is in the political landscape. There is a lot of deliberately inaccurate news strategically placed on social media platforms, which is weaponized to advantage some politicians and disadvantage others. Unfortunately, we also have too many leaders undermining the important role of a free press by calling its investigative work and revelatory scoops 'fake'. More than ever, people need to be discerning with the messages they are being fed, and must cultivate trust with only reputable news sources. Leaders also need to have an honest presence on social media platforms because it's the first place the public and media will go to for information. For this reason it's vital that you look after your online presence.

A great deal of your success in office also comes down to the advisors and press secretaries who work with you. Find someone who has a track record in public relations or communications who can help you write, plan and execute both a hard and 'soft' media marketing plan. It's useful and sometimes essential (depending on how high you have climbed the ladder) to have expert advice on growing your personal brand. The advice I have always given senior politicians is to share more about who they are and tell their personal story as a way to connect with voters. In short, I am a huge proponent of using so-called soft media. Politicians receive a bigger and more positive response by doing so.

> 66 Although the term 'soft news' was originally synonymous with feature stories placed in newspapers or television newscasts for human interest, the concept expanded to include a wide range of media outlets that present more personality-centred stories."
> —*Encyclopaedia Britannica*[8]

In the 1990s I worked extensively with an opposition leader that I greatly admired, who later became New Zealand's Prime Minister. Some of Helen Clark's staff members were initially very reluctant about my insistence that soft media could help cultivate a new relationship with the public as they were introduced to a more nuanced and softer person rather than the one-dimensional politician the media liked to portray her as. I wanted to humanize her and allow the public to know the warm, witty woman I knew.

For the pages of a women's magazine, I organized an article with a photograph of a confidant woman looking warmly into the eyes of the camera while playing piano, which was her hobby. Her hair was soft, wavy and cut in a stylish bob. Her professional make-up accentuated her high cheekbones and she looked comfortable and content in casual clothing. According to some, Helen had never been represented like this in the media before because she had only ever had photos that were formal and traditional.

She could see the importance of including her appearance as a part of her personal brand. But she could see that the constant scrutiny placed on her image was distracting to voters. Reluctantly, Helen agreed to take professional advice and realized that she didn't have to sacrifice her integrity in order to create this new image. I had the challenge and honour of creating a soft media campaign where she was enabled to look open, happy and relaxed in magazine shoots. This captivating photograph told readers more about her life away from politics, and the photo has had a long shelf life and lives on in an excellent book,

Helen: Portrait of a Prime Minister, by broadcaster and journalist Brian Edwards.

Soft media was once a foreign concept, but these days anyone in the public eye can use social media platforms as a form of soft media to share a little bit more about who they are. We see more partners, children and pets with politicians and celebrities than we've ever seen before. Public figures all around the world now invite people into their homes, which is ironic because they often guard their privacy, but they need their followers and supporters to see a more human side to them. And this is where authenticity is important. All human beings have hobbies. You might like to ride motorbikes off-road or go fly fishing in the wilderness. You might love trekking in Nepal or writing poetry. Whatever your hobby is, let people know what you're made up of.

Most people don't dine out on domestic policy, political jargon or international trade. They want to hear more about you and know what you can do for them. And, more importantly, they want to relate to you. Your job as a leader is to build relationships with potential followers and supporters, and there has never been an easier time to reach out to them.

Humour

Chatty radio interviews or podcasts as well as comedy appearances are also great soft media vehicles, where public leaders can show a more human and humorous side of themselves. But beware! You must be really comfortable going off the cuff and also have a natural and easy sense of humour as well as being okay with being poked fun at.

The Obamas are class performers in these soft media scenarios. Worth looking at are two comedy series in which they individually appeared. While still serving as President of the United States, Barack Obama agreed to participate on Jerry Seinfeld's digital comedy series *Comedians in Cars Getting Coffee*. Seinfeld is comedic royalty but Obama, with his ease and genuinely credible comic timing, held his own and the episode went viral because of its great entertainment value.

Michelle Obama was possibly even more impressive in my view when she appeared with UK comedian James Corden on his segment 'Carpool Karaoke' in July 2016. She agreed to be on the show to promote her global initiative for female education called 'Let Girls Learn'. She sang, boogied and cracked jokes and in my opinion nailed the performance. It's no surprise that she has been one of the most popular First Ladies and was also such a political asset to her husband.

Another great example of soft media working wonders for participants is a podcast for the BBC from December 2017, conducted by Prince Harry with Barack Obama nearly a year after he left office. Obama spoke surprisingly and somewhat reassuringly about his 'serenity' while at the inauguration of Donald Trump in January 2017, and also talked lovingly and admiringly of his wife and their partnership. Again, this was great soft media in action, as it made both Obama and Prince Harry look and sound great in the eyes and ears of listeners. And, of course, it went viral so was a slam dunk with positive and maximum exposure.

Always on show

Having a public career that requires you to be on-form all the time is stressful no matter how healthy and strong you are. You are in a microscopic fish bowl no matter where you go or what you do. Going to the supermarket for most of us is no big deal, but for well-known people in some countries it's not an easy task. They are stopped by strangers, constituents or fans wanting a selfie or are being surreptitiously filmed by anyone with a phone for possible sale to a gossip site or magazine. There are enormous sacrifices to make. Ask the partner, husband, wife or lover of any celebrity, prime minister, politician or mayor and they will tell you that it's not a normal life. I know this first-hand because I have spoken with many partners of my high-profile clients and I've observed their frustration, anger and heartache. Most of them tell me 'the partner takes it the hardest' when relating how their loved ones react to the abuse and slander that too often appears in the media.

Case study: politicians

A good example of 'always having to be on show' is when Hillary Clinton continued to work despite having chronic pneumonia in 2016 when she was running for President. Media footage showed her almost collapsing. This was not good timing on her campaign trail and what made it worse was that the public weren't told she was unwell. Many politicians fall sick due to the strain of the job and a lack of sleep. Unfortunately, most continue to carry on even to the detriment of their health. As we have discussed elsewhere in this book, in my opinion part of being authentic is to show your vulnerability. It's more honest to tell the truth and show emotion. Often politicians are criticized for breaking down in tears or admitting that they're unwell — but I believe that if you show your feelings and share the truth of a gruelling schedule, you are more likely to connect with people because you are being human. Being 'stiff upper lipped' or concerned about appearances suppresses who you really are in that moment.

Canada's Prime Minister, Justin Trudeau, is a political leader who is unafraid to show his emotions in parliament. He has shed tears unashamedly on many occasions in full view of the media. Personally, I found his speech and apology for Canada's decades-long 'state sponsored, systematic oppression and rejection' of its LGBT people moving and sincere. In the middle of his speech I watched this elegant, handsome man remove a small white handkerchief from out of his trouser pocket and wipe away his tears. Behind him, a colleague also had tears falling down her cheeks. 'The number one job of any government is to keep its citizens safe, and on this, we have failed LGBT communities and individuals time and time again,' declared Trudeau during the formal apology.[9] As a trained actress, my point of view is that you can't fake tears unless you are a practised professional — so Trudeau's tears were genuine.

In my opinion, voters are not interested in you pretending to be strong when you're not. They are interested in you being human. However, there are others who would suggest that politicians need to show resilience. Voters are looking for leadership and they expect their leaders to stand up and be sympathetic and reassuring yet strong and in control. A senior male politician once challenged me on my views on the subject of vulnerability and said, 'Crying in public — especially a man — is still seen as a sign of weakness and should be avoided at all costs! People want to know their politicians — leaders — are in control and emotional fragility can often be seen as a sign of weakness.' We agreed to disagree on this point. My belief is that whether you are a new candidate or the seasoned leader of a political party, don't be afraid to be real, no matter what the circumstance is.

Heeding the call

So, let's say the decision has been made and you are going to apply for a leadership role or stand for election. Your new career is about to begin. My first question to you is simply: Why? With your skill set and talents, why are you choosing to heed the call to serve in a public role rather than perform in another career?

If you genuinely want to be a change-maker, stand up for people's rights and leave the world a better place (the more altruistic reasons for public service), then the work begins to cultivate a personal brand. You must fully invest in this work, so that your personal brand is strong and reflects who you are — a real, authentic human being. It's important to remember that it is not just about understanding policy; it's about understanding yourself so you can create change. You also need to honestly survey your past and ask yourself if there is anything that you have not dealt with that could be discovered and used to damage your brand. Seek advice and work out a strategy to resolve any past issues and publicly talk about them. There are communications experts who can guide you. Also, to be authentic you have to own and take responsibility for all your past actions, the good and the bad. This is a bold step and, if managed well, can be seen by the public as strong rather than weak.

You have to have a thick skin to take the hard knocks, and there will be hard knocks. But on the flipside, we need you. We need people who are prepared to do a good job for our communities and not be too bruised by people chipping away at their self-confidence. As Michelle Obama said, 'Do not bring people into your life who weigh you down. And trust your instincts ... good relationships feel good. They feel right. They don't hurt. They're not painful. That's not just with somebody you want to marry, but it's with friends that you choose. It's with the people you surround yourself with.'[10]

What do you stand for in life?

66 The most successful brands are built around what's real."

—*William Arruda, author and personal brand guru*[11]

Communicate what you stand for and be unwavering. I once worked regularly with an emerging public leader who drove three hours for every training session with me. He struggled to articulate what it was he stood for and I kept on pushing him to dig a bit deeper. I knew about the extraordinary things he'd done in the community and about his personal life, and yet he was unable to give voice to them. I felt he hadn't really named his values out loud. His narrative was all about policy, and there wasn't a story about why he wanted people to vote for him. It took me two sessions to really get out of him who he was and what his values were. In the end, he was elected. He later told me that the most valuable lesson he learnt in our training sessions was to succinctly express what he was fighting for: being a strong advocate for fairness and dignity for all and fighting for those without a voice in his community.

From my experience, if you understand what your values are, it will be easier for you to put a stake in the ground and stand up for what you believe in. Door-knocking may not be your most favourite thing to do (especially if the door is slammed loud and fast in your face), but your self-belief will help you to not take it personally. Being born in the country where suffragettes paved the way for women to have the vote has taught me that anything is possible if you fight for what you believe in.

Motivation and mentoring

66 We should always have three friends in our lives. One who walks ahead whom we look up to and follow, one who walks beside us, who is with us every step of our journey. And then one who we reach back for and bring along after we've cleared the way."

—*Michelle Obama, First Lady of the United States, 2009–17*[12]

No one can teach you how to be authentic. In striving to be a change-maker, watching and learning from the actions of successful leaders is beneficial especially before campaigning or applying for a high-profile position. Who has a strong visible brand? Why? Who stands out and what did they do that was different? What can I learn from this influential person whom the public respects?

Here are two tips I hear often from seasoned leaders, about creating a personal brand:

- Be innovative.
- When you don't know something, admit it. Then make it your business to find out.

Most of the clients I work with say that getting started in the business was helped by support from mentors. So, if you hear the call to leadership, scout around for an inspirational figure and then ask yourself why that person generates your respect. Does she fight for the poor and disadvantaged? Does he stand up for human rights and call things as he sees them? Did she help protect the environment or save an endangered species? Did his fiscal policies seem fair and innovative to you? Did she orientate the business towards a social responsibility strategy?

You might find a mentor in the annals of history and read biographies or accounts of history when one man or woman's voice saved a country or even the world from the brink of disaster. Or you might even get in touch with an inspirational public official to discuss your ideas and a pathway to public service. What have you got to lose? Everybody, even a national leader, was at one time starting out with big ideas and a fire in the belly. If they are a true representative of the people, they should be open to speaking with you, to sharing and mentoring.

Trust

66 Contrary to what most people believe, trust is not some soft, elusive quality that you either have or you don't; rather, trust is a pragmatic, tangible, actionable asset that you can create."
—*Stephen M.R. Covey, American author*[13]

In a 2018 Gallup survey, nurses were nominated as the most trusted of all professionals, with 82 per cent of respondents declaring them trustworthy. Right at the bottom of that list were business executives, with only 16 per cent of Americans finding them worthy of being trusted. This shows that business leaders really need to think about their personal brand and reputation.

In my opinion, there is unfairness in business executives having a bad reputation because it's usually only a few that spoil it for the rest.

From my research, sexual harassment and expense fraud are the two most frowned-upon sins. Both are illegal, and both, in my view, should be prosecuted if proven true. When scandal breaks, what inevitably happens is that the public feels betrayed, often not just by the offenders but the community as a whole.

When people have been nominated to lead, a covenant of trust is formed between elector and elected, and the feeling of betrayal occurs when this is broken. Whether they're running a political party, a high school, a mayoral office or even a global board, when scandal hits, there's a pervasive sense of broken trust.

Megan Barry was appointed the first female mayor of Nashville in 2015. At the time she took office she was known for her integrity and her good work ethic. However, she resigned in 2018 after pleading guilty to felony theft related to an extramarital affair with a city employee, her bodyguard. At the time there was a mixed reaction from the public, ranging from outrage to support. Some of her followers forgave her and compared her with her male counterparts in office, who had been rumoured to have had extramarital affairs. Others wanted her to resign immediately because their trust had been broken. Whatever the reaction, Megan Barry had no choice but to resign, stating that she felt she should hold herself to the high standard that voters deserved of her. She also noted that she is a human, she made a mistake, and she was disappointed in herself.

It really comes down to your honesty and your reputation. It's up to all leadership parties to expect the highest standard from all who serve in their name in order to keep public trust.

Power

> 66 Power can burn. No one can give us power if we aren't part of the process of taking it, we won't be strong enough to use it."
> —*Gloria Steinem, American author*[14]

Anyone who puts power over principle is, in my opinion, getting it wrong. They are seeking a leadership role for the wrong reasons, looking for status rather than service. A true leader must have certain qualities. Some people look for power because it serves them and their interests but most often the role of the leader is actually to serve the people. It is not to misguide or betray them.

It is a privilege to serve your country, your state or your local community. When I am listening to interviews on the radio I cringe when I hear racist or sexist remarks made by people in positions of power who ought to be role models. It has the same effect on me when I listen to older middle-aged men talking about women as second-class citizens, objects or sexual play things. I also can't abide religious leaders being moralistic and bigoted. While I accept others will have different views from mine, I am angered when I hear elected officials deliberately trading in divisive and hate speech. No population has ever truly been served by the tactic of divide and conquer. Those who use that strategy generally have a short public service shelf-life.

The public doesn't expect you to be a saint. But your ethics and morals will be scrutinized. You are being paid to do a job. Look at world leaders who have a dishonourable reputation. What have they done to create this? Usually they don't follow through on their promises, they put others down or deliberately lie to the public, only to be exposed later. Dishonourable leaders or elected officials are like day traders who don't put the people first, instead choosing the power of the position and the thrill of a quick victory.

While having mentors is important, it's also fundamental to surround yourself with people who you trust will give honest feedback on your behaviour. Brian Lowery, Professor of Organizational Behaviour at Stanford University, says, 'What I strongly suggest is, as your power grows you have people to have you check your own behaviour. Don't rely on yourself as a good person to check your behaviour because you could end up missing what is going on.'[15]

Getting the outfit right

❝ The costume affects your posture, affects your walk, how you hold yourself, and how you breathe. The costume makes you deliver."

—*Richard Madden, Scottish actor*[16]

Every leader needs to look professional and smart, and clothing plays an important part in shaping your personal brand. Many of the high-profile clients I have worked with have been resistant to styling because they wanted to stay true to themselves. But matching your brand with your clothing doesn't mean that you are being somebody else. Usually, after a couple of shopping sessions, my clients eventually see the importance of image in relation to personal branding. You might have the biggest brain in the world and be very media savvy, but if you dress badly, that's all people will remember.

If you are thinking about applying for a prominent leadership position, start managing your wardrobe now. It should be part of your preparation and training because you are on show all the time. I have worked with a number of emerging leaders and it's interesting to notice how once in the top job they dress if not impeccably, certainly more attentively. Clearly, their career ascent has forced them to realize that clothing does matter.

❝ To thine own self be true."

—*William Shakespeare*[17]

Be true to yourself. The wonderful thing about clothing is that you can still express your personality through a jacket, tie or pair of shoes. If you are speaking to a business audience or dignitaries you need to wear corporate attire but you can still incorporate certain elements that express your personality. You could wear a vibrant, patterned tie or an elegant silk scarf. There is a traditional rule with television which is to avoid stripes because they can occasionally strobe (this is where the screen appears to shake and it can be distracting for audiences).

It's also crucial, especially if you secure the help of a stylist, that the clothes you wear are an extension of you. Don't feel you have to look a certain way or allow an image consultant to convince you to wear the opposite of what you like. You will just end up feeling uncomfortable and the audience or people you meet will interpret this as untrustworthy. I had a client, a former senior member and front-bencher of the UK Labour party, who hated skirts and dresses. I briefed the professional dresser to look for certain types of pant suits with soft lines that made my client feel comfortable but at the same time smart and 'feminine'. I even persuaded her to get a professional manicure — something she wasn't used to — because, as I explained, when she was addressing parliament her gesturing was seen on camera, and if her nails and hands were smart, people wouldn't be distracted from her message.

Learn from others. Look at impressive leaders who dress well. What is it about his or her clothing that you admire? Why does he or she always look smart and stand out? Is it to do with colour, accessories or style?

I award Barack Obama, 44th President of the United States, the gong for the best dressed politician in the world! Put him alongside his fashionable wife and you've got a stylish power couple. What I really liked about Barack Obama's style while he was in office was that he would often have his shirt sleeves rolled up, giving a more casual appearance while still looking smart and professional. It sent the message to audiences that he was ready to get stuck in and work for the people. This shows that no matter what your status is, you can wear clothes to express yourself while still looking powerful and polished.

My advice is always to buy a few high-quality pieces that can be worn multiple times. Quality fabric lasts forever, so don't buy cheap clothing. When I am helping a client with their clothing the first thing I do is study their wardrobe. I look at what is missing and what works well. After this, we go shopping and I make suggestions. The one thing I learnt very early on is to recommend comfortable clothing. In my earlier career, I once insisted a politician wear high heels to a garden event. On the day, her heels sank into the grass and she was forced to awkwardly walk around on her toes. She has never forgotten it and we laugh about it to this day. She also likes to joke with her former colleagues, 'Whatever you do, don't let Maggie take you shoe shopping!'

Plan your wardrobe well in advance for specific events to remove the anxiety and stress. How often have you heard a friend saying, 'I have nothing to wear'? You don't need this extra burden when you are trying to focus on writing and performing a speech. An image consultant friend taught me to have a typed-up wardrobe planner and fill it in for the client so they know what to wear for the whole week. It really comes down to being organized, prepared and proud of your image. Many people I know have their colours done and I think this is a very useful exercise. For example, my colours are autumnal: burnt orange, browns, mustards and olive greens. This might seem trivial but it can make it easier to narrow down your clothing choices while working out what suits you. It's also helpful to take note when people stop you and say, 'That colour really suits you'.

Wear the clothes now for the career you want. If you aspire to a prominent leadership position, for example a school principal or a board chair, start dressing for the job you want. Don't wait and definitely don't show up to meetings looking scruffy and expect people to respect you. What is your clothing saying about your personal brand? Ask a friend or a colleague who you trust to describe your style. Is it quirky, conservative, stylish, classical or edgy? Clothing has a language, so be very clear about what you want your clothing to convey.

The same rules apply for everyone. When people listen and watch you they are taking in the entire package. What does this mean? They are looking at what you are wearing, listening to what you are saying and observing your body language. Wear what is appropriate for your audience. Research the culture you are going to visit. If you are going to a school fair, you might feel more comfortable in jeans and an elegant shirt. However, if you are going into a corporate environment always wear business attire or smart garments that make you look professional. You don't have to dress conservatively in a black suit — you can still be true to your personality — but keep in mind who your audience is. Our opinions are shaped by what we see and I guarantee that when people get home after seeing you, among other things they will talk about what you were wearing.

What conversation do you want people to have about your appearance? Always keep that firmly in your mind!

We have choices in life and we can choose to make decisions that will destroy our reputation and our personal brand, or we can stand back and think about the future, think about how we want to be perceived when we are older and make healthy choices that keep our followers respecting us. Your personal brand is constantly evolving and the only person in control of that is you. Leaders come and go but those who leave bigger footprints put their communities before their own desires.

Be the leader who leaves a legacy that you and your loved ones can be proud of.

Parting words

In trying to find a pithy way to conclude this book and bring it full circle so that you can feel ready to take your brand into this world and lift it to new heights, I need not look any further than the two words which adorn the cover — being you. That's my instruction and your mission. Use this book to discover new ways to strengthen your work, your business and your relationships based on the beliefs and values close to your heart. Being you is more important than being liked by someone else.

I acknowledge you for looking after your reputation, figuring out how you are perceived, investigating ways to re-think things when necessary and for taking the time to explore who you are as a brand in the world and why that should matter. Dig deep with this enquiry into your reputation and take steps to recreate your personal brand on solid foundations.

Keep on asking that confronting question, 'Am I being authentic?' And, as you examine this question, imagine what it could look like if you truly were interacting in the world with a more genuine you and more genuine message. Pause on this for a minute, because in that understanding you can give action and voice to the real you. Therein lies your personal brand.

Always remember that, like everything in life, your brand will evolve just as spaciously and daringly as you do. I disagree with the expression, 'people don't change'. People do change — every day — and watching transformation unfold is quite simply a joy. I am not the same person I was a year ago when I started writing this book and an unexpected but much welcomed consequence of committing to this work is that I have found myself contemplating my own personal brand and examining how I can keep growing it and better communicate it.

One of my heroines is Swiss–American psychiatrist Elisabeth Kübler-Ross. She expressed the truth about human nature so vividly when she wrote, 'People are like stained-glass windows. They sparkle and shine when the sun is out, but when the darkness sets in, their true beauty is revealed only if there is a light from within.'[2] You are the only person who can turn that light on. And in flicking the switch, you become a brighter personal brand that will inspire your family, friends, followers and fans. Being you is about personal liberation. No longer do you have to pretend or wear a mask that hides the true person that you are. If there is one thing you can change about yourself to become a better person, then do it. Act now with determination and make a break with anything that is holding you back and not in step with your values.

Social media guru, activist and chief operating officer of Facebook, Sheryl Sandberg, has strong views on personal branding. Like many, she isn't a fan of the term. She is famous for saying, 'Don't package yourself'. In other words, she's advocating to just speak honestly, factually and from your own experience. 'We're not packaged,' suggests Sandberg. 'And when we are packaged, we are ineffective and inauthentic. I don't have a brand, but I do have a voice.'[3] I respect Sheryl Sandberg's distinction and see it as an important point to unpack and probe. You are not Coca Cola or Nike — these are commercial world brands marketed to sell products. People are not products, but we sell services which are products, and we need to do this in a truthful way. We are complex human beings with feelings, thoughts and emotions. We are judged by our reputation and actions and how we come across in meetings, speeches and in our everyday comportment.

So if you have come to the end of this book (I'm sincerely grateful to you for reading it) and are still uncomfortable with the term personal branding, that's fine. It's really a question of semantics. What is crucial, though, is that you move forward standing for what you believe in, allowing authentic expression of your mind, heart, values, passions and imaginings — and communicate that boldly. I personally believe it's better to embrace personal branding as both a phrase and a concept to help you grow your business, manage your reputation and harness your potential in life and work. Allowing the idea of yourself as a personal brand urges and dares you to stand out.

Being yourself is the opposite of following a social media trend, a step-by-step tip formula sheet or clichéd, safe talking points. We find out about what makes us grow by making mistakes and going easy on ourselves and others, with compassion and humanity, especially when we or they trip up. Having the courage to be vulnerable is what will also orientate you towards a true voice and a true personal brand. Whatever you do, savour the moments that make a defining difference and dare to touch the lives of everybody you encounter as you navigate your own unique path.

Do this by BEING YOU.

Acknowledgments

I would like to thank my wonderful publishing team at Exisle, who has become family to me over the thirteen years we have known and worked together.

Gareth St John Thomas, my publisher, I acknowledge you for having my back and coming up with the title *Being You*. We have been brainstorming this book on personal branding for three years and I'm grateful to you for believing in me. Without you this book would not be on the shelf or in the digital world. Thank you for mentoring and challenging me with this project and guiding me to broaden my audience.

Anouska Jones, thank you for the extensions, your positive attitude and teaching me how to improve the manuscript. I am grateful for your

Aussie 'straight talking' and no nonsense style and manner. This is our second book together and I value our working relationship.

Karen Gee, thank you for your excellent editing. I have learnt so much more about how to turn your manuscript into your best book, with your insightful feedback. This has been an easy online relationship across the ditch, so much so that I feel that I know you and have found a new friend. You really are an author's dream come true. I will forever be grateful. Thanks to you, my book will have a long shelf life.

Carole Doesburg, at Exisle, thank you for the fast turnaround when getting my books out on time all over the country and putting up with my last-minute and unreasonable requests to get supplies to clients on time. You are irreplaceable and I appreciate you greatly.

To the sales and publicity team at Exisle, bravo and thank you for spreading the word about *Being You*.

Giulia Sirignani, my trusted and inspiring friend and writing coach, based in Milan, who's always on the end of the phone when I need you. We have lived and breathed everything there is to know about personal branding. Thank you for watching over my work, crafting my words when I got stuck and giving me honest feedback, sometimes tough but always constructive, on every page and chapter. Your coaching inspires me to grow as a writer and I could not have done this without your belief and dedication to the work and my own personal brand. You are a valued Fresh Eyre Associate and we have lots more great work to do together.

Stephanie Clews, the hardworking and calming influence who has been working for me for over ten years in London and New Zealand. Thank you for managing me and my business. You go beyond the call of a personal assistant's duties and are the unsung hero behind the scenes. This is the third book we have worked on together and I simply could not have finished the race without you. You hang in there through all seasons as we toil under the demands of running a small and growing business. I don't have enough thank yous in me to aptly express my appreciation.

Professor Marilyn Waring, Dr Gill Greer, Susan Kegley, Minister Stuart Nash and broadcaster John Hudson. My dearest friends with great minds and big hearts, thank you for reading and casting a focused eye over a challenging chapter about leadership and giving me honest written feedback. Heartfelt gratitude to all of you for your massive investment when you are all time poor. You individually are all powerful and strong personal brands in the public eye and I am blessed to have your moral and professional support. I salute your generosity, kindness and honesty.

Allie Webber, our content queen at Fresh Eyre, co-trainer and long-lasting business pal and friend. Thank you for allowing me to share your expertise in this book. You are the absolute wise owl in my business and always ready to thrash out ideas and challenge me to be a better person. You are authentic to the core, the most genuine and inspired teacher and live your values day by day! Interviewing me about personal branding at the start of this project was the spark that lit the fire in my belly! Thank you for broadening the Fresh Eyre pool of clients and for helping to create the privilege of working with high-performing athletes and refugees.

Lorae Parry, thank you for bringing your extraordinary comedic skills to our workshops. Our clients love your voice sessions and your creative talents know no bounds. When the technology breaks down, you are calm and carry on. Your friendship and wise counsel means the world to me.

Vivien Sutherland Bridgwater, my bestie! Thank you for reminding me to be proud and not focus on the struggle of writing a book. You are the most loyal, faithful and true-hearted friend and your brand shines so brightly, reaching to the far ends of the globe. Thank you for being my ambassador and opening business doors that never close. You are family to me.

Sue Walter, thank you for providing a quiet sanctuary to write in your nurturing home in Tunbridge Wells, Kent — my home away from home. Your kindness towards me and unfailing support made it possible to begin work on my book. You are the finest example of a dynamic leadership brand and I'm inspired by your courage and grace. You mean the world to me.

Margaret Koski, Fresh Eyre's credit controller. Thank you for your positivity. You always find a solution to every problem and you remind me weekly on the phone not to sweat the small stuff!

To all my Fresh Eyre associates, I acknowledge you for living and breathing the Fresh Eyre values and bringing your individual styles to our clients. The family continues to grow and your creativity and expertise strengthens the Fresh Eyre brand every time you perform on our various stages.

To the four men in my life — my four dear brothers. Eddie Eyre, my oldest brother who lives next door and with whom I experience family every day — thank you. You listen without judgment and are my sanity check and rock. Your compassion and service to all those you attend to restores my faith in humanity.

Tony Eyre, a writer in your own right, thanks for continuing to give me professional advice about the business. You speak the truth and keep me on my toes!

Michael and Rob, my younger brothers, you are my greatest ambassadors and I am forever grateful for your unconditional love and support. Our family is a tight team.

To my mother, Jean Violet Eyre, the sincerest person I have ever known. This is my first book without you in the world. You are an example of what authenticity is. You were my best critic and my big love and

I honour your memory in my work while committing to share your stories so they live on.

Lastly, thank you to all of my clients around the globe who have allowed me to use their amazing stories of growth in the book. I am still a student in this lifetime of learning how to be a more authentic human being. You remind me of who I am and help shape my personal brand every day. I never take it for granted how you share your vulnerability and allow me the privilege of working with you. Thank you for trusting me to show you how to strengthen and build your personal brands.

Endnotes

Introduction

1. Quinn, J. (2015), Walking on the Pastures of Wonder: John O'Donohue in conversation with John Quinn, Veritas Publishing, Dublin.
2. www.theodysseyonline.com/12-dr-seuss-quotes-get-you-through-life

1. What is a personal brand?

1. Simon Mainwaring: www.brainyquote.com/quotes/simon_mainwaring_494020
2. e.e. cummings: www.brainpickings.org/2017/09/25/e-e-cummings-advice/
3. *Oxford English Dictionary*: https://en.oxforddictionaries.com/definition/authentic
4. *Oxford English Dictionary:* https://en.oxforddictionaries.com/definition/reputation
5. William Burroughs, advice to Patti Smith: www.goodreads.com/quotes/917268-build-a-good-name-keep-your-name-clean-don-t-make
6. Sharon Isbin: www.minnpost.com/arts-culture/2014/11/guitarist-sharon-isbin-instead-traveling-stars-she-became-one
7. Roger Federer: timelesstennis.blogspot.com/2013/12/tennis-quote-of-day-roger-federer.html
8. Roger Federer: www.tennisworldusa.org/tennis/news/Roger_Federer/26624/roger-federer-africa-is-a-magical-continent-we-want-to-give-children-a-better-life-/
9. Roger Federer: https://timesofindia.indiatimes.com/sports/tennis/wimbledon-2017/mirka-key-to-my-success-roger-federer/articleshow/59572207.cms
10. Roger Federer: www.ibtimes.com.au/roger-federer-absorbs-losses-faster-faster-age-36-1559723
11. https://twitter.com/edsheeran/status/122630364886859776?lang=en
12. Jasmine Helmsley: https://ruthlittleeskimo.wordpress.com/2016/05/12/the-art-of-the-matter/

2. How to define your personal brand

1. Mohandas K. Gandhi: www.goodreads.com/quotes/50584-your-beliefs-become-your-thoughts-your-thoughts-become-your-words

2. Barbara De Angelis: www.goodreads.com/author/quotes/72891.Barbara_De_Angelis

3. Anthony Robinson: https://quotefancy.com/quote/922692/Tony-Robbins-Your-life-changes-the-moment-you-make-a-new-congruent-and-committed-decision

4. Dr Brené Brown: www.goodreads.com/quotes/746519-vulnerability-is-the-birthplace-of-love-belonging-joy-courage-empathy

5. Byron Katie: www.habitsforwellbeing.com/its-not-your-job-to-like-me-its-mine

6. Christopher Germer: www.huffingtonpost.com/.../self-compassion-benefits_us_573c8ff9e4b0ef8617

7. Dr Kristin Neff: www.huffingtonpost.com/kristin-neff/self-compassion_b_865912.html

8. Dr Kristin Neff: www.huffingtonpost.com/kristin-neff/self-compassion_b_865912.html

9. Dr Kristian Neff: www.curtrosengren.com/why-self-criticism-doesnt-work-and-what-does/

10. Christopher Germer and Dr Kristian Neff: self-compassion.org/wp-content/uploads/2017/01/Finlay-Jones2016.pdf

11. Dr Kristian Neff: www.nzherald.co.nz/lifestyle/news/article.cfm?c_id=6&objectid=12035058

12. Martha Stewart: www.thedailybeast.com/martha-stewart-in-the-dock-over-macys-lawsuit-i-did-my-time

13. Douglas Adams: www.brainyquote.com/quotes/douglas_adams_148569

14. Anita Roddick: https://quotefancy.com/quote/1388512/Anita-Roddick-I-want-to-define-success-by-redefining-it-For-me-it-isn-t-that-solely

15. Joseph Campbell: www.brainyquote.com/quotes/joseph_campbell_378372

16. David Ogilvy: www.pinterest.com/pin/78390849737181789/

17. Kristi Russo: www.pinterest.com/kristinarusso11/

3. Talent spotting your target market

1. Nate Elliot: www.affinio.com/blog/2017/03/21/10-audience-insights-quotes-every-marketer-should-read/

2. Chris Karcher: https://quotefancy.com/quote/946622/Chris-Karcher-Integrity-is-choosing-your-thoughts-and-actions-based-on-values-rather-than

3. Simon Sinek: www.goodreads.com/quotes/668292-people-don-t-buy-what-you-do-they-buy-why-you

4. Katherine Johnson: www.brainyquote.com/authors/katherine_johnson
5. Author unknown: www.thequotablecoach.com/old-ways-wont-open-new-doors/
6. Albert Einstein: www.brainyquote.com/quotes/albert_einstein_122232
7. Katherine Barchetti: https://allauthor.com/quotes/96643

4. Digital presence: Your shop window

1. Jeff Bezos: www.forbes.com/sites/danielnewman/2015/10/13/customer-experience-is-the-future-of-marketing/#1c9fcfc5193d
2. Jeff Rum: https://sjinsights.net/2014/09/29/new-research-sheds-light-on-daily-ad-exposures/
3. Susan Cooper: www.inc.com/jim-belosic/17-quotes-that-will-make-you-a-better-social-marketer.html
4. Erin Bury: https://markitgroupmedia.wordpress.com/2013/12/05/great-quotes-about-social-media/
5. www.facebook.com/marketingAPAC/posts/985868748172474
6. Ben Shaw and Jack Colchester: www.warc.com/newsandopinion/opinion/peoples_attention_is_out_there_we_just_need_to_earn_it_not_buy_it/2554
7. Bonnie Sainsbury: www.commpro.biz/importance-social-media-professions-inspirational-quotes/
8. Don Crowther: www.pinterest.com/pin/395824254743043324/
9. Laura Filton: www.pinterest.com/pin/428545720784497974/
10. Viveka von Rosen: https://books.google.co.nz/books?isbn=1118461347

5. The power of storytelling

1. Ira Glass: www.goodreads.com/quotes/1317166-great-stories-happen-to-those-who-can-tell-them
2. Susan Gurelius: www.actioncommunications.com.au/2017/05/21/brand-story/
3. Adele: www.brainyquote.com/quotes/adele_421406
4. Isabel Allende: www.goodreads.com/quotes/348638-you-are-the-storyteller-of-your-own-life-and-you
5. M. Scott Peck: www.brainyquote.com/quotes/m_scott_peck_392902
6. Madeleine L'Engle: www.goodreads.com/quotes/64058-when-we-were-children-we-used-to-think-that-when

6. Presentation skills to build your brand

1. Lauren Clement: www.nzherald.co.nz/business/news/article.cfm?c_id=3&objectid=11840878

2. Lauren Clement: www.nzherald.co.nz/ddb-new-zealand/news/article.cfm?c_id=1504323

3. Sir Richard Branson: https://quotefancy.com/quote/898836/Richard-Branson-Your-brand-name-is-only-as-good-as-your-reputation

4. Laurence Olivier: www.theguardian.com/stage/2012/sep/21/stephen-fry-stage-fright

5. Susan Chritton: www.huffingtonpost.com/susan-chritton/personal-brands_b_2729249.html

6. Judy Apps: www.goodreads.com/author/show/3100115.Judy_Apps

7. James William Coleman: https://books.google.co.nz/books?isbn=1614293759

8. *Oxford English Dictionary*: www.oxforddictionaries.com/de/definition/englisch_usa/fight-or-flight

9. Jodi Picoult: www.goodreads.com/quotes/175364-when-you-re-different-sometimes-you-don-t-see-the-millions-of

10. Carmine Gallo: https://books.google.co.nz/books?isbn=1466837276

11. Don Ranly: www.ragan.com/how-do-you-produce-riveting-content-in-the-digital-age/

12. Walt Whitman: www.brainyquote.com/quotes/walt_whitman_146850

13. Oprah Winfrey: https://awakenthegreatnesswithin.com/50-inspirational-oprah-winfrey-quotes-on-success

14. Oprah Winfrey: www.accredited-times.com/2018/01/12/oprahs-golden-globe-speech-greatest-time/

15. Sidney Poitier: www.brainyquote.com/quotes/sidney_poitier_600544

7. Networking your personal brand

1. Elizabeth Asquith Bibesco: www.closepartners.com/E/StichtingMarketing.pps

2. *Oxford English Dictionary*: https://en.oxforddictionaries.com/definition/network

3. Alan Lakein: www.brainyquote.com/quotes/alan_lakein_154655

4. Susan C. Young: www.goodreads.com/quotes/search?page=55&q=effort+and+success

5. Roy T. Bennett: www.goodreads.com/quotes/7553679-listen-with-curiosity-speak-with-honesty-act-with-integrity-the

6. Ben Dattner: www.careerattraction.com/networking-with-depression-and-anxiety

7. Catriona Pollard: www.linkedin.com/pulse/5-personal-branding-strategies-every-entrepreneur-needs-moses-edemba/

8. Albert Einstein: www.brainyquote.com/quotes/albert_einstein_383803

9. Ronald Reagan: www.usnews.com/news/articles/2008/01/17/the-actor-and-the-detail-man

10. Steve Jobs: www.businessinsider.com.au/what-john-sculley-wishes-he-knew-when-he-became-apple-ceo-2016-3?r=US&IR=T

11. Maya Angelou: www.brainyquote.com/quotes/maya_angelou_392897

12. Emdad Khan: www.linkedin.com/pulse/10-common-networking-mistakes-avoid-suman-jung

13. Marne Levine: www.brainyquote.com/quotes/marne_levine_850359

14. Stephen Hawking: www.goodreads.com/quotes/469784-quiet-people-have-the-loudest-minds

15. Cain, S. (2013), Quiet: The power of introverts in a world that can't stop talking, Penguin, London, p. 121.

16. Cain, S. (2013).

17. Cain, S. (2013).

18. Bruce H. Lipton: www.goodreads.com/author/quotes/52035.Bruce_H_Lipton

8. Styling your brand

1. Tom Peters: www.huffingtonpost.com/marc-lesser/branding-you-when-you-don_b_763033.html

2. Linus Sebastian: www.lifehacker.com.au/2015/08/im-linus-sebastian-of-linustechtips-and-this-is-how-i-work/

3. Susan Gunelius: https://aytm.com/blog/research-junction/introduction-to-brand-strategy-part-1

4. Daniel Bliley: www.bebee.com/producer/@javierbebee/why-personal-branding-is-a-crucial-part-of-being-successful-in-today-s-connected-world...

5. Amber Hurdle: www.goodreads.com/author/quotes/16512488.Amber_Hurdle

6. Eva Chen: www.brainyquote.com/quotes/eva_chen_798208

7. Coco Chanel: www.brainyquote.com/quotes/coco_chanel_382612

8. Miuccia Prada: www.brainyquote.com/quotes/miuccia_prada_438975

9. Jacob Share: http://www.personalbrandingblog.com/let-a-personal-branding-accessory-boost-your-brand/

10. Gianni Versace: www.brainyquote.com/quotes/gianni_versace_338929

9. TED Talks: A tool in building your personal brand

1. Chris Anderson: https://mannerofspeaking.org/2010/02/20/excellent-interview-with-chris-anderson-of-ted/

2. Dr Brené Brown: www.goodreads.com/quotes/556598-maybe-stories-are-just-data-with-a-soul

3. Smitha Singh, 2015: www.youtube.com/watch?v=d70jOSN6TJc

4. TEDx Speaker Guide: https://storage.ted.com/tedx/manuals/tedx_speaker_guide.pdf

5. Dr Brené Brown: https://quotefancy.com/quote/777786/Bren-Brown-At-the-end-of-my-life-I-want-to-be-able-to-say-I-contributed-more-than-I

6. Kristi Hedges: www.forbes.com/sites/jacquelynsmith/2013/08/13/how-to-give-a-great-speech-3/#501a61326696

7. Carmine Gallo: https://books.google.co.nz/books?isbn=1466837276

8. Henry David Thoreau: www.brainyquote.com/quotes/henry_david_thoreau_166869

10. Leadership in the limelight

1. Theodore Roosevelt: www.goodreads.com/quotes/7-it-is-not-the-critic-who-counts-not-the-man

2. Robert Kennedy: www.goodreads.com/quotes/705426-each-time-a-man-stands-up-for-an-ideal-or

3. Brendan Cox: www.independent.co.uk/news/uk/home-news/jo-cox-trafalgar-square-memorial-42nd-birthday-husband-children-dead-killed-tributes-a7095591.html

4. Madeleine Albright: www.huffingtonpost.com/marianne-schnall/madeleine-albright-an-exc_b_604418.html

5. Kristin Linklater: www.azquotes.com/quote/918768

6. Peter Brook: https://quotefancy.com/quote/1107717/Peter-Brook-The-work-of-rehearsal-is-looking-for-meaning-and-then-making-it-meaningful

7. Margaret Thatcher: www.brainyquote.com/quotes/margaret_thatcher_131837

8. Encyclopaedia Britannica: www.britannica.com/topic/soft-news

9. Justin Trudeau: http://www.dailymail.co.uk/news/article-5126283/Canada-PM-apologizes-oppression-LGBTQ-communities.html

10. Michelle Obama: https://obamawhitehouse.archives.gov/the-press-office/2011/05/25/remarks-first-lady-event-elizabeth-garrett-anderson-students

11. William Arruda: www.forbes.com/forbes/welcome/?toURL=https://www.forbes.com/sites/williamarruda/2016/12/13/why-consistency-is-the-key-to-successful-branding/&refURL=https://www.google.com/&referrer=https://www.google.com/

12. Michelle Obama: www.goodreads.com/author/quotes/2338628.Michelle_Obama

13. Stephen M.R. Covey: www.movemequotes.com/quotes-from-the-speed-of-trust/

14. Gloria Steinem: www.feminist.com/resources/artspeech/interviews/gloriasteinem.html

15. Brian Lowery: https://qz.com/746643/the-more-powerful-you-are-the-less-you-should-assume-youre-right/

16. Richard Madden: www.brainyquote.com/quotes/richard_madden_705204

17. William Shakespeare: www.enotes.com/shakespeare-quotes/thine-own-self-true

Parting words

1. Lao Tzu: www.brainyquote.com/quotes/lao_tzu_137141

2. Elisabeth Kübler-Ross: https://en.wikiquote.org/wiki/Elisabeth_Kübler-Ross

3. Sheryl Sandberg: wwww.inc.com/tanya-hall/sheryl-sandberg-isnt-a-fan-of-the-personal-brand.html

Index

Index